The Mixing Bowl

─o/o/o─

Our Lady's Hospice & Care Services

The Mixing Bowl is dedicated to the men and women
who gave this book its voice, and its heart.

First Published in Ireland in 2011 by
Our Lady's Hospice & Care Services
Harold's Cross
Dublin 6W
info@olh.ie
www.olh.ie

The Mixing Bowl
ISBN: 978 0 9541728 1 7

Photography supplied by www.istockphoto.com
Book design, layout and typesetting by DaveDarcy.com
Illustrations by Sarah Brownlee
Printed in Ireland by www.indianfield.ie
Print brokerage by Caroline Kennedy, Indian Field Print Management & Solutions

www.olh.ie

Contents:

Chapter 06: Afternoon Tea 69

Chapter 07: Charming Cakes 81

Chapter 08: Cookies & Buns 93

Chapter 09: Entertaining Friends 103

INTRODUCTION

When I walk into my kitchen today, I am not alone. Whether we know it or not,
none of us is. We bring fathers and mothers and kitchen tables, and every meal we
have ever eaten. Food is never just food. It's also a way of getting at something else:
who we are, who we have been, and who we want to be.
— Molly Wizenberg, A Homemade Life: Stories and Recipes from My Kitchen Table

It is with considerable pleasure that I write this introduction to a cookbook that
tells the stories of lives well lived and the food that accompanied them.

Cooking evokes such feelings in us all with some of the most powerful memories
we have often involving food: the smells of the kitchen at home as you come in
from school, the memories of the family mealtimes or trips to favourite relatives
who were great cooks, and the wonderful delectations laid on for tea.

One of the most popular activities in Our Lady's Hospice & Care Services is
cookery, with many of our residents actively participating. There is also huge
interest in our daily menus and a wonderful range of tastes exhibited in the
requests for different food by our clients.

These days there is a growing interest in recipes from days gone by and looking
to the past for renewed inspiration for traditional cooking. Many popular chefs
are producing books that seek to use the wisdom of past culinary practices to
develop a new way of enjoying food that gives a nod to the expertise of an older
generation. Our contribution to this important gathering of culinary knowledge
is this special book.

The contribution to this book from clients in our Older People's Service is a
reflection of their lives and is to be valued as our oral history. The book reflects
a culinary knowledge and history that has an important part in our lives today.
It is a wonderful opportunity to learn how to make many dishes and cakes that
so many buy ready-made in shops today. Many of the recipes have passed down
through the generations; from mother to daughter, from grandfather to grandson,
reflecting not just the sustenance shared but the relationships enjoyed.

Producing this cookbook has brought great joy to many people. We hope it
brings the same to you.

Mo Flynn
CEO, Our Lady's Hospice & Care Services

FOREWORD

It all began with an apple sponge.

Seán, an 80 something-year-old client I admitted two years ago gave me his recipe for it, a tenderly moist and sweet pudding, to try at home. It was delicious and something happened then. More and more recipes started to arrive from the clients for me to try. There was shepherd's pie, brown bread, chocolate cake... a collection of treasured recipes was steadily growing. Each complementing this burgeoning collection in different ways. I didn't realise at the time I was embarking on a rewarding journey which would eventually lead to the publication of this book, *The Mixing Bowl*.

Every single one of these recipes was kindly given to the book by the residents and clients of the Extended Care Unit (ECU) and The Community Reablement Unit (CRU) at Our Lady's Hospice & Care Services, Harold's Cross. In the recipes - ingredients, methods and tips - lie years of life experience, wisdom and wit that we sometimes overlook in our elderly community.

This journey has given me, and the many wonderful staff at the hospice, a glimpse into the lives of the men and women we care for everyday. People whose rich and varied lives have contributed so much to the world we live in today; a farmer, a world-class dressmaker, a father-of-ten, a war veteran, a homemaker, a talented school teacher. Some were well enough to tell their stories, while others were not so fortunate. In these instances their stories are told through the voices of loved ones: a son, a daughter, a wife or perhaps a friend. For this we are very grateful.

There are stories of friendship, family gatherings, declarations of love and often times, hardship. *The Mixing Bowl* includes recipes from contributors who are no longer with us. It is my hope that their family and friends take comfort in this book, as here lies their legacy.

The Mixing Bowl is so much more than just a recipe book, it is a glance into the lives (and kitchens) of our residents and clients here at the Hospice. These individuals have very generously shared with us a little taste of their lives. Let us reminisce together and savour every delicious bite.

Dr Sheela Perumal,
Medical Officer, Older Peoples Services

A MESSAGE FROM NEVEN MAGUIRE

As someone who began life as a young boy cooking under the shadow of my mother, I understand the value of cooking simple ingredients well.

The recipes in this book give us a snapshot of an Ireland when the kitchen was the hub of the house and the waft of whatever was cooking on the hob or in the oven, was what brought family and friends together.

Each recipe evokes a wonderful snippet from the life of its contributor and tells us that the food we eat is about so much more than sustenance. It is about sharing lives and pleasurable moments with friends and family, the memories of which are fondly held and nurtured for the rest of our lives.

I am delighted to be associated with this book and its contributors, all clients of the Older People Services at Our Lady's Hospice & Care Services, Harold's Cross. There are many gems in here for you to try out and enjoy and I would like to thank all contributors and their families for sharing them so generously.

Enjoy!

Neven Maguire

ACKNOWLEDGEMENTS

A very special thanks to the following
individuals who have made this book
possible:

Recipes and recollections recounted
by Rose Kevany

Contributors and recipes were
recruited by Monica Devine and
Jane Brownlee

Recipes tested by Gemma Hynes

Recipes and interviews edited by
Emma Walsh

Illustrations by Sarah Brownlee

Graphic design by Dave Darcy

Coordination support by
Suzanne Johnston, Criona Cullen
and Sabrina Kevany

Recipes typed by Avril Hannigan

Chapter 01

Breakfast Delights

—o/o/o—

Traditional Brown Bread

by Alice Gibson

INGREDIENTS:

14oz/400g wholemeal flour

7oz/200g plain white flour

1oz/25g margarine

½ tsp salt

1 tsp sugar

1 tsp bread soda

15fl oz/425ml buttermilk

This brown bread is a must at every breakfast table and takes literally minutes to prepare. Slathered in butter, it's the perfect thing to accompany the great Irish fry.

Serves: 8—10 / *Preparation time:* 15 minutes / *Cooking time:* 45 minutes

METHOD:

1 Preheat the oven to 200°C/400°F/Gas mark 6.

2 Put the wholemeal flour into a good sized bowl and sift in the plain white flour on top.

3 Mix together. Then rub in the margarine with your fingers and add the salt, sugar and bread soda. Mix well together.

4 Make a well in the centre of the dry ingredients and pour in the buttermilk. Mix everything together with a wooden spoon or large knife. Add more milk if necessary until you have a nice soft (but not too soft) dough.

5 Place the dough on a floured surface and begin to knead lightly until all the cracks are removed.

6 Shape into a round loaf and place on a floured tray. Score it across the top with a knife.

7 Bake in the oven for ½ hour. When the bread is nicely brown, reduce the heat to 190°C/375°F/Gas mark 5 and turn bread over if necessary. Continue to bake for another 15 minutes.

8 To check when the bread is done, tap the base of the loaf and if it sounds hollow then it is ready to come out of the oven.

9 Leave to cool on a wire tray and enjoy.

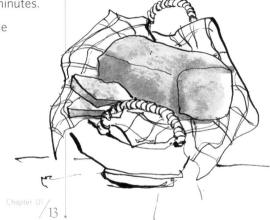

Bubble & Squeak

by Gerry O'Callaghan

Ingredients:

2lbs/1kg mashed potatoes

1 medium onion, diced

8oz/250g finely diced cooked cabbage

4 tbsp butter

Salt & pepper

Serves: 6 / *Preparation time:* 5—10 minutes / *Cooking time:* 15 minutes

Method:

1 Melt the butter in a large non-stick frying pan on a medium heat, add the onion and fry until soft.

2 Add the cabbage and mash and fry until everything is thoroughly reheated.

3 Season with salt and pepper before serving.

Tip: Serve with a fried egg on top. Bubble & Squeak can be made up of whatever leftover ingredients are available to you. The fact that it is different every time adds to its charm!

Gerry's mother always made a big roast on Sundays and after the dinner was dished up the remains of the potatoes, peas and cabbage would be put into the cabbage pot, mixed together with good butter and put aside for the next day. On a Monday morning the big cast iron pan would be taken out and the Bubble and Squeak would be started.

In the O'Callaghan house this Monday morning speciality would have to stretch to feed ten children and two adults! Each child would get a portion of the Bubble and Squeak with a freshly fried egg on top, doled out in order of age, from the eldest first. With a family this large meals always had to be shared out fairly to ensure happy spirits!

Sunday Morning Fry

by Gerry O'Callaghan

INGREDIENTS:

2 pork sausages	1 egg	1 slice of bread
2 back rashers	1 tomato	*Multiply the ingredients for more servings as appropriate*
1 slice of black and white pudding	3—4 mushrooms	
	Beans	

Serves: 1 / *Preparation time:* 5 minutes / *Cooking time:* 10 minutes

METHOD:

1 First, get your pan on the heat, medium to high, and add some butter or cooking oil. Fry the sausages until brown on all sides then place them on a tray and put into a warm oven while you get on with the rest.

2 Slice the tomato in half and fry it, add it to the oven with the sausages to keep it warm.

3 Next, add the rashers and pudding to the frying pan. When they are ready to be turned over, add your sliced mushrooms to the pan then turn them over and cook everything together.

4 Heat your beans in a pot on the hob while you continue to cook the rashers, pudding and mushrooms.

5 When the rest of your fried ingredients are ready, add them to the tray in the warm oven and fry your slice of bread in the pan, absorbing all the flavours left over from the previous items.

6 Clean your pan with kitchen paper and add some new oil and then fry your egg.

7 When the egg is ready, take all of your fry from the warm oven and serve on a warm plate with plenty of tea and toast.

Tip: With a few alterations or additions i.e. liver, pork chops or lamb chops, hamburgers etc. this can make a great mixed grill suitable for any substantial meal.

A career in the army taught Gerry a plethora of utilitarian skills that he employed over the years running a family and home, often on a shoestring budget. After serving abroad for over eight years he returned to Dublin where he married and moved into a tiny flat in Richmond Hill with his wife. The minute kitchen, painted shiny jade green, boasted a Belfast sink (good for sharpening knives) which did double duty for laundry and dishes, and filled with cold water was the ideal fridge. The children learned fast peeling techniques from their dad who, ever the military man, inspected the skins for thickness which he equated with waste. The peelings were sold to the Pig Woman who kept swill; a woman who Lee Dunne, in his notorious book Goodbye to the Hill, *claimed was his mother! There was a fireplace in the sitting room, where the cinders were preserved and blown into life with a few lumps of coal. A press in the corner stored food on the top shelf and coal in the bottom drawer. There was a wood factory nearby, and Gerry collected ends which he cut with a hatchet into 12-inch sticks and sold for a penny or two. Gerry had no hesitation about cooking, scrubbing, or boiling nappies, he did whatever it took to make things work for his family, and with ten children welcomed to the family it's a good thing he did!*

This recipe is for the ultimate meal to start a busy family day.

Drop Scones

by Seán O'Riain

Ingredients:

8oz/225g flour	Pinch of salt	1 egg
½ oz/15g caster sugar	1 tsp baking powder	10fl oz/300ml milk

Makes: 12–15 scones / *Preparation time:* 10 mins / *Cooking time:* 10 mins

Method:

1 Mix all the dry ingredients together.

2 Make a well in the middle of the dry ingredients, drop the egg in, add a little milk and stir well, drawing in the flour as you mix.

3 Blend until all the milk is mixed in.

4 Fry tablespoonfuls of the batter at a moderate heat in oil or margarine until lightly browned. These are delicious served warm with butter and jam or, for an extra treat, with sliced banana and maple syrup.

Seán's career as a Pharmacist kept him very busy and though his wife was a wonderful cook he always liked to make time to cook for her on his days off. These drop scones were a speciality of his.

In fact, it was through his career that he actually came to meet, and fall in love with, his wife.

It was early on in his career when a lovely young woman came into his pharmacy complaining of a pain in her tummy. 'Where abouts is the pain?' Seán enquired. 'Here,' she said, pointing to the sore spot in the centre of her stomach. 'Oh thank goodness', he replied, 'you're very lucky'. 'Why is that?' she responded worriedly. 'Well, if the pain was only on one side you'd be in danger', he answered. 'Oh no', she exclaimed, 'what would that mean then?' With a cheeky smile Seán replied; 'it would mean your heart was aflutter!' Six months later they were engaged and, as the best stories go, they lived happily ever after.

Reibekuchen

(Potato Pancakes)

by Rolf Baumgarten

INGREDIENTS:

5lbs/2.25k potatoes	3 cloves of garlic	Oil for frying
4 medium yellow onions	1 tbsp salt	
4 eggs	1 tbsp of flour	

Makes: 12 / *Preparation time:* 25 minutes / *Cooking time:* 10 minutes

METHOD:

1 Coarsely grate the potatoes and onions or use a food processor to shred them. Add the salt.

2 Drain the excess liquid from the grated potato and onion mix in a sieve or colander, trying to reserve as much potato starch as possible. Discard the liquid.

3 Add in the eggs and the flour and mix well.

4 Place a non-stick frying pan over a medium to high heat and pour in just enough oil to cover the base of it.

5 When the oil is hot, drop heaped tablespoonfuls of the potato mixture onto the pan and flatten with the back of the spoon.

6 Cook until golden brown, approximately 3 minutes each side.

7 Place each cake on a paper towel to soak up the excess oil before transferring to the oven to keep warm.

8 Replenish the oil and repeat until all the mixture is gone.

9 Serve with apple sauce, sour cream, autumn jelly or mayonnaise.

Rolf was a dab hand at making these traditional German potato cakes. He remembers working at outdoor festivals, in his student days, often with four pans on the go making up to 16 at a time, intermittently cooling himself with chilled beers as he juggled everything at once. To stick with tradition serve these with apple puree and a sprinkle of nutmeg.

Autumn Jelly

by Rolf Baumgarten

INGREDIENTS:

2lb/900g mixed
blackberries, rosehips
and elderberries

2lb/900g crab apples
1lb/450g granulated
sugar

4 or 5 sloes (to help the
setting process)

Makes: 5 pots / *Preparation time:* 2—3 hours / *Cooking time:* N/A

METHOD:

1 Wash the fruit and heat slowly in a large pot with 15fl oz/
425ml of water until the fruit is soft and all the juice has
run out of it.

2 Strain the liquid through a piece of muslin or a tea towel
and collect in a large bowl. This can take several hours so
you may wish to leave this to strain overnight.

3 Measure the resulting liquid and for every pint of liquid
collected you will need 1lb of sugar.

4 Pour the liquid and sugar into a large pot and heat very
slowly stirring continually until all the sugar has dissolved.

5 Turn up the heat and boil the liquid for about 10 minutes
or until setting point has been reached. You can test the
setting point by putting a teaspoonful of the liquid onto
a saucer. When it is cool push it with your finger and if a
wrinkle forms on the surface it is ready.

6 Pour the jelly into warmed jars, cover and leave to cool.

*Around Rolf's house the fields were
rampant with blackberries, rosehips,
crab apples, elderberries and sloe
berries. He and his wife Maureen
would collect the fruit and boil up
the whole lot to make their favourite
Autumn Jelly. This jelly can be enjoyed
in so many ways and keeps well
throughout the seasons.*

Chapter 02

Soups, Starters & Light Lunches

Salmon Quiche

by Eileen Sheehy

INGREDIENTS:

PASTRY:
6oz/175g flour

3oz/75g margarine

Pinch of salt

Cold water

FILLING:
4oz/110g salmon (tinned, or alternatively you can use fresh, cooked salmon)

2oz/50g grated cheddar cheese

½ oz/15g margarine

½ onion, finely chopped

2 tomatoes

2 eggs and 1 egg yolk

Salt and pepper

½ pint/ 300mls cream or milk

This quiche makes the perfect summer lunch served with a fresh garden salad.

Serves: 4—6 / *Preparation time:* 20 minutes / *Cooking time:* 25—30 minutes

METHOD:

1 Preheat the oven to 200°C/400°F/Gas mark 6.

2 Sieve the flour and salt into a bowl. Add the margarine in small pieces, and then rub it into the flour with the tips of your fingers until the mixture resembles fine breadcrumbs.

3 Add enough cold water (approximately 3 tbsp) to bind it all together and mix to a fairly stiff dough. Turn the dough out onto a floured board and knead lightly.

4 Roll out the dough with a floured rolling pin and line a 9 inch (23cm) flan ring with it. Ensure the flan ring is lightly greased so the shell casing doesn't stick.

5 Set the ring on a baking tray and line the pastry shell with greaseproof paper, then fill with baking beads or uncooked rice and bake in the centre of the oven for 12—14 minutes. This will prevent the crust from becoming soggy when you add the filling later.

6 After 12 minutes, remove the greaseproof paper and the baking beads/rice, brush the base of the pastry case with egg wash and put back in the oven for 3—4 minutes, until golden.

7 Next, melt the margarine and gently fry the onion in it for 1 to 2 minutes. Put the tomatoes into a bowl, pour boiling water over them, leave for one minute and then remove the skins, slice them and remove the seeds.

8 Arrange the onion, tomato and salmon in the baked flan case. Beat the 2 eggs and egg yolk together in a bowl, add the cheese and cream and season well. Pour the egg mixture into the pastry shell on top of the onion, tomato and salmon.

9 Place in the oven and bake for 25 minutes, serve with a fresh garden salad.

Salmon Cakes

by Maureen Goggin

INGREDIENTS:

1 medium can of salmon

3 large potatoes, boiled and mashed

2 medium eggs, beaten

2 spring onions/or 1 finely chopped onion

1 tsp parsley, finely chopped

1oz/25g flour

Salt and pepper to taste

Makes: 8 / *Preparation time:* 20 minutes / *Cooking time:* 30 minutes

METHOD:

1 Mix all of the ingredients in a bowl and shape the combined mixture into small flat circles about ½ inch thick.

2 Shallow fry them in olive oil or sunflower oil on a medium heat until golden brown on both sides.

3 Serve hot with rocket salad and fresh lemon or lime juice.

Tip: This recipe can also be made with tuna instead.

Maureen's daughter Mary submitted the recipes in this book that her mother used to make for their family on her mother's behalf. Mary said that Maureen used to make up many of her recipes as she went along. She possessed a natural talent for cooking and loved improvising and experimenting when it came to food. She would pick up an idea from a magazine or neighbour or on the back of a store-bought ingredient and add to it to make it her own. She would marinate pork chops in orange juice and whatever else she found in the fridge, or mix smoked haddock and smoked cod, as she said herself; 'sure the fish will never know the difference by then!' She would bring life to day-old mashed potato by adding cream cheese and chives and perhaps some salmon. This is a classic 'Maureen recipe'.

Vegetable & Tomato Soup

by Nuala Breheny

INGREDIENTS:

2 large onions

2 large carrots

1 small potato

¾ stick of celery

One portion of any other kind of vegetable you like e.g. peppers, parsnips

2 heaped tbsp of red lentils

1 tin of tomatoes (400g)

1 tbsp vegetable oil

2 pints vegetable stock

Salt and pepper to taste

Serves: 6—8 / *Preparation time:* 15 minutes / *Cooking time:* 1 hour

This great recipe can be adapted to suit almost any taste. It makes a tasty, hearty soup that's handy to keep in the freezer. If you don't like tomatoes, simply don't add them, you'll still have a great vegetable soup without them.

METHOD:

1 Chop all the vegetables into small pieces.

2 Heat the oil in a heavy based, large saucepan and toss the vegetables in the heated oil for 1—2 minutes, until coated.

3 Add the hot stock and lentils and cook on a medium heat so it simmers lightly for approximately ¾ hour.

4 When cooked, add the tomatoes and the juice from the tin and heat the entire soup through.

5 Liquidise the soup or put it through a food processor until thick and creamy.

6 Serve with a dollop of natural yoghurt for an extra creamy taste.

Tip: If you find your soup is too thick, simply add small amounts of water to it until it develops the right consistency.

—— o/o/o ——

Annie's Broth

—— by Jean Kinch ——

INGREDIENTS:

7oz/200g carrots	7oz/200g turnips	7oz/200g stewing beef, cubed
7oz/200g parsnips	7oz/200g leeks	2 pints/1 litre beef stock
7oz/200g celery	7oz/200g peas	Salt and pepper to taste
7oz/200g onions	1oz/25g orange lentils and barley, washed	1 tsp chopped parsley

Serves: 4 / *Preparation time:* 20 minutes / *Cooking time:* 2 hours

METHOD:

1 Finely chop all the vegetables and sauté in some olive oil in a large saucepan.

2 When the vegetables are nice and soft, add the lentils, beef and parsley.

3 Increase the heat slightly and continue to cook until the meat is thoroughly browned.

4 Add the stock and bring the whole broth to the boil and simmer to reduce the liquid for about 2 hours.

5 Serve with toasted country brown bread.

Jean grew up in Belfast and barely remembers the hardships of finding enough food to cook during WWII because she spent all her free time around the corner, in the luxury of 'Gran's kitchen'. Her devotion to her grandmother was lovingly returned as she learned from her the 'mysteries of cooking'. Her Gran used to make her own bread and butter during the War and popular staples back then during those hard times were champ, corned beef and cabbage, and a glass of buttermilk.

Jean recalls eating lots and lots of potatoes in her grandmother's house; 'I used to be able to eat four or five big floury potatoes in one sitting' she remembers. Jean herself always enjoyed cooking good, plain hearty meals like corned beef, roast beef, steak and onions, but most of all, she adored this broth. This recipe for Annie's Broth is, nevertheless, her mother's concoction. She used to go to the greengrocer to get 'veg for stew' and come home with a newspaper-wrapped collection of fresh vegetables that would make a delicious broth that would last for two days. The delicious scent of steaming broth is the smell of home for Jean.

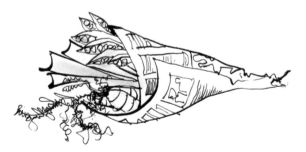

Hot Spinach Dip

by Noreen Buckley

Ingredients:

8oz/225g soft cream cheese

3fl oz/75ml mayonnaise

1 small chopped onion

1 tin of chopped spinach (frozen spinach, cooked according to the directions on the packet works equally well)

1oz/ 25g grated parmesan cheese

Squirt of lemon juice

Serves: 6—8 / *Preparation time:* 10 minutes / *Cooking time:* 30 minutes

Method:

1 Preheat the oven to 180°C/350°F/Gas mark 4.

2 Mix all the ingredients together in a bowl and pour into a ceramic, ovenproof dish.

3 Bake in the over for 30 minutes.

4 Serve as a dip with crackers or raw vegetables.

Noreen left her home in Kerry at the tender age of 16 to move to the United States. She settled with her uncle in the Bronx, New York. She arrived full of hopes and dreams, thinking life was going to be full of opportunity; 'I was going to pick money off the streets' she recalls with amusement at her own naivety. She was frightened that she would not get through her first job interview but was hired quickly to work in Shrafft's Restaurant on 42nd Street, the same restaurant Audrey Hepburn dined in, in the film Breakfast at Tiffany's. The restaurant appeared in many Hollywood films and was known for its fantastic food. Luckily Noreen got to eat all her meals there. In the film Kramer vs. Kramer, Dustin Hoffman's son eats Shrafft's chocolate chip ice cream instead of his main meal, and Noreen could well understand why!

She learned a lot about food and cooking in the United States and her culinary style is a mixture of North American cuisine with traditional Irish dishes. This hot spinach dip is inspired by the food from this iconic restaurant.

Focaccia Soda Bread

by Íde Ó Háinle

INGREDIENTS:

1lb/450g plain white flour

8fl oz/225ml buttermilk

1 tsp bread soda

1 tsp salt

Sun blushed tomatoes (quantity to taste)

Olives (quantity to taste)

Feta cheese (quantity to taste)

Fresh or dried Rosemary (quantity to taste)

Serves: 8—10 / *Preparation time:* 10 minutes / *Cooking time:* 30 minutes

METHOD:

1 Preheat the oven to 200°C/400°F/Gas mark 6.

2 Mix the flour, bread soda and salt together and add the buttermilk, ¾ of the sun blushed tomatoes and the olives.

3 Mix well with a wooden spoon until they come together to a dough, then using your hands knead the dough thoroughly for about 2 minutes.

4 Roll out to roughly 1 inch/2cm thick and place on an oiled baking tin or Swiss roll tin measuring approximately 25 x 35cm.

5 Press your thumb into the top of the dough intermittently to create dimples and decorate with the remaining tomatoes, feta cheese and sprigs of rosemary.

6 Drizzle lightly with olive oil and bake in the oven for 30 minutes.

7 Enjoy with a glass of wine and some Italian opera!

Working as a resource teacher in a primary school gave Íde the opportunity to pursue and impart to others her two great passions in life, music and cooking.

In Scoil Neasáin she taught music to all the pupils in all classes from Junior Infants right up to Sixth Class, and no one was left out. Determined to find a way to meld her two great passions together, Íde introduced cookery classes as well as music classes in Sixth Class. Under her tutelage the students would prepare brown scones and soups, make their own fresh hummus and pesto, make coconut, mint and toffee slices and special occasion cakes, such as a ring cake for Mother's Day.

Thus she taught both music and cookery to her eager pupils, among whom were her own two daughters, Fionnuala and Caoimhe, and inspired in them a great love for these two sensory delights.

Tá sí ar scor anois, agus í go sona sásta ag ullmhú béilí blasta dá fear céile ionúin, Cathal.

Thai Crab Cakes

by Marie Nolan

Ingredients:

11oz/300g crab meat	1 hot red chilli, seeded	Few sprigs of fresh coriander
1oz/25g white breadcrumbs	1 tsp grated fresh ginger	Juice of ½ small lime
3 spring onions, chopped	1 tsp nam pla (a fish sauce available from Asian supermarkets or most standard supermarkets)	Flour for dusting
2 garlic cloves, crushed		Salt and pepper to taste
2 tbsp low-calorie mayo		

Makes: 6 cakes / *Preparation time:* 30 minutes / *Cooking time:* 10 minutes

Method:

1 Put the crab meat, chilli, spring onions, garlic, ginger, coriander, nam pla, mayonnaise and lime juice into a blender. Blitz in short bursts until combined then tip into a bowl.

2 Stir in the breadcrumbs, season, then cover and chill for 20 minutes.

3 Divide the mixture into 6 portions and shape into round patties. Dust lightly with flour.

4 Lightly oil a non-stick frying pan and place over a medium heat. When hot add the crab cakes and cook for 3—4 minutes each side until golden brown. Carefully turn over so they keep their shape.

5 Serve the crab cakes hot with sweet chilli sauce, boiled rice and a crisp salad.

When Marie took early retirement in 1988 she was unsure of what she would do to fill her formerly busy days. However, a love of cards and a sociable nature led her to form, together with 3 friends, a bridge circle and a new pastime was born. She took lessons and, competitively minded, aimed to be the best in Ireland. However, instead of the competition circuit she found new best friends and a strong passion for a great game. Now she is spending more time playing cards than the span of her working life; that says something good about retirement. For Marie, bridge is a great game because it exercises the mind, brings the joy of winning and, better still, good laughs with good friends.

Her favourite pastime is to spend a couple of hours with her friends, playing 'no teapot, no china' card games. This means no high society preparations are allowed; she prefers mugs of tea or coffee and simple easy food.

Chapter 03

Amazing Mains

—o/o/o—

Lamb Tagine with Cous Cous

by Neven Maguire

INGREDIENTS:

2 tbsp paprika

1 tbsp each ground coriander and turmeric

2 tsp each ground cinnamon and cumin

1.5kg (3lb 5oz) lamb shoulder, well trimmed and cut into 4cm (1 1/2in) chunks

2.5cm (1in) piece peeled root ginger, chopped

4 garlic cloves, chopped

3 onions, roughly chopped

2 tbsp olive oil

600ml (1 pint) tomato juice

600ml (1 pint) chicken stock

50g (2oz) toasted flaked almonds

225g (8oz) Medjool dates, cut in half and stones removed

2 tbsp clear honey

Maldon sea salt and freshly ground black pepper

Couscous, to serve

Greek style yoghurt and fresh coriander leaves, to garnish

Neven Maguire has kindly donated this recipe to our book.

'I like to make my tagines a little richer than is traditional in Morocco. This involves browning the meat, frying off the spices, reducing the sauce and cooking it all gently in the oven with the delicious Medjool dates. The flavour of this tagine only improves with time, just leave it to cool completely, then place in the fridge for up to two days.'

Neven Maguire

Serves: 4—8 / *Preparation time:* 30 minutes* / *Cooking time:* 2 hours

METHOD:

1 Mix together the paprika, coriander, turmeric, cinnamon, cumin and one teaspoon of the pepper in a large bowl, then tip half into a small bowl and set aside. Add the lamb to the large bowl and coat in the spices. Cover with clingfilm and chill overnight.

2 Preheat the oven to 160C (325F), Gas mark 3. Place the garlic, ginger and onions into a food processor and pulse until finely minced. Heat a large, heavy-based casserole dish. Add half of the oil and brown off the marinated lamb in batches. Add the remaining oil to the pan and then add the onion mixture, cook for a few minutes until softened but not coloured. Stir in the reserved spice mixture and cook for another minute or so until well combined.

3 Pour the tomato juice and stock into the pan and then add the browned lamb with the honey, stirring to combine. Bring to the boil, cover and transfer to the oven. Cook for 1 hour, then stir in the dates and cook for another hour until the lamb is tender and sauce has thickened and reduced. Season to taste.

4 Arrange the tagine on plates with the couscous. Scatter over the toasted almonds and then garnish with a dollop of the Greek yoghurt and coriander.

* Preparation time: 30 mins (& overnight marinating)

Shepherds' Pie

(Gluten Free)

by Mary Groves

Ingredients:

1lb/450g round steak mince

2 sticks of celery, finely chopped

1 carrot, finely chopped

2 shallots, finely chopped

2 cloves of garlic

Mixed herbs

A little vegetable oil

2 tsps tomato puree

3 or 4 potatoes, boiled and mashed

Gravy:

2 tsps gravy mix (gluten-free)

1 beef stockpot (gluten-free)

½ pint/ 300ml of hot water

Mary is a coeliac so has had to learn to cook without using wheat, barley, oats and rye; ingredients she avoids to prevent symptoms of the condition. She cannot touch white flour and has learnt a lot about cooking gluten free since joining the Coeliac Society. Her recipes are all designed for coeliac sufferers.

Serves: 2 / *Preparation time:* 10 minutes / *Cooking time:* 1 hour

Method:

1 Preheat your oven to 180°C/350°F/Gas mark 4

2 In a pan, gently fry the carrots, celery and shallots in a little vegetable oil until soft. Add the mince and mixed herbs and continue to fry until the mince is browned and cooked through. Add the tomato puree. Leave on a low heat whilst you make the gravy.

3 For the gravy; combine the gravy mix, any brand will do, with the stock pot and the water on a medium to high heat and whisk thoroughly until lump free.

4 Add the gravy to the meat and vegetable mix and stir thoroughly. Then transfer to an ovenproof casserole dish, cover with foil, and cook in the preheated oven for 30 minutes.

5 While this is cooking in the oven, make your mashed potatoes by boiling your potatoes for about 20 minutes, or until soft and fluffy when pierced with a knife. Mash them well (you can add a dollop of butter for extra creamy mash).

6 Remove the meat dish from the oven and top with the mashed potato.

7 Return to the oven and cook for a further 20 minutes or until the potatoes are nicely browned.

Lasagne

by Sister Margaret Madden

INGREDIENTS:

1lb/450g round mince beef

2 large carrots

1 onion

½ red pepper

2 sticks of celery

5 or 6 mushrooms

1 clove of garlic, crushed

2 x 400g tins of tomatoes

1 tsp tomato puree

1 tbsp tomato ketchup

Lasagne sheets

1 tsp of dried basil

1 bay leaf

Parsley

Salt and pepper to season

CHEESE SAUCE

4oz/110g margarine

4oz/110g flour

2oz/50g cheese

2 pints/1 litre milk

1 medium sized onion (studded with approx 8 cloves)

1 egg yolk

Sister Margaret is a great believer in the health benefits of fresh and natural food. Her youth is full of memories of food made from natural, local ingredients. As a young woman she loved going out looking for berries and herbs, cycling on her old Raleigh bike, with the family dog, Ship, for company. Lasagne is one of her favourite recipes; for her it's the epitome of good food made from wholesome fresh ingredients and packed full of flavour.

Serves: 4—6 / *Preparation time:* 45 minutes / *Cooking time:* 45 minutes

METHOD:

1 Preheat the oven to 180°C/375°F/Gas mark 5.

2 Peel and stud the onion with cloves and drop into the milk to infuse for the white sauce.

3 Chop the carrots, celery, mushrooms and peppers into small pieces. Sauté the onions in olive oil in a large pot at a low temperature, add the crushed garlic and chopped vegetables and continue to sauté at a high heat. Add the round mince and fry until browned. Then add the tinned tomatoes, puree and ketchup and bring to the boil.

4 Turn down the heat and simmer for about half an hour until the celery and carrots have softened. Add the herbs 5 minutes before the end.

5 Make the cheese sauce by melting the margarine in a smaller saucepan and then adding the flour. Mix well until smooth. Add the milk (remove onion first) and then add the cheese and egg yolk, mixing all the while on a low heat and season. When thickened, remove from the heat and leave aside.

6 Remove the bay leaf from the Bolognese and transfer half of the sauce to an ovenproof dish.

7 Layer the lasagne sheets on top and add another layer of bolognaise. Layer with lasagne sheets again and pour the cheese sauce over the top. Cook in the oven for about 45 minutes, until golden brown and bubbling.

Lamb Hot Pot

by Breda McTigue

INGREDIENTS:

4—6 gigot chops or 1lb 2oz/500g stewing lamb

14oz/400g sliced potatoes

2 onions, chopped

3—4 carrots, diced

2 pints/1 litre beef stock

Salt and pepper to taste

2 tbsp chopped parsley

Serves: 4 / *Preparation time:* 25 minutes / *Cooking time:* 1 ½ hours

METHOD:

1 Preheat the oven to 200°C/400°F/Gas mark 6.

2 Brown the meat in some oil in a heavy bottomed saucepan on a medium to high heat.

3 Layer the cooked meat and vegetables in an ovenproof dish.

4 Layer the slices of potatoes over the top and pour the stock over the entire contents.

5 Season well with salt and pepper.

6 Bake for 1 ½ hours in the preheated oven.

7 When cooked, remove from the heat, leave to rest for a few minutes and garnish with chopped parsley before serving.

Breda was a 'live life to the full' kind of person. She had a wicked sense of humour and believed that laughter was always the best medicine. As a young woman she was a very active person; she played sports, excelled at camogie and was a huge GAA fan. Professionally, she became a hotel and restaurant manager and spent 21 years working in Sherry's Restaurant, where she lavished care and attention on all of her customers. She was very much a people person; she enjoyed socializing, parties and made every second count.

Breda was diagnosed with a brain tumour in her 50s, and given three months to live, but she proved everyone wrong. She lived for another eight years, on the determination, love and care of her husband, Tom. In fact, it was only when she fell ill that Tom asked her to marry him, though they had been living together for 21 years, she found this hilarious! They were married in Beaumont Hospital chapel in an extremely poignant and moving ceremony.

When Breda came to the Hospice, she began collecting recipes and keeping them for her best friend Marion. She was particular about measuring her own ingredients, carrying out the recipe to the full and being in control of where the recipe was taking her. In her life too, she remained independent, and in charge of her destiny to the end.

Potato & Leek Bake

by Rita Dempsey

INGREDIENTS:

5fl oz/ 150 ml vegetable or chicken stock

9oz/250g potatoes sliced

2 leeks

2 rashers, lean

Knob of butter

Serves: 2 / *Preparation time:* 10 minutes / *Cooking time:* 30 minutes

METHOD:

1 Preheat the oven to 200°C/400°F/Gas mark 6.

2 Put the stock into a heavy bottomed saucepan and bring to the boil.

3 Add the sliced potatoes and leeks and cook for 5 minutes. Drain the stock off to keep for later.

4 Fry the bacon in butter until crispy.

5 Put the cooked bacon in an ovenproof dish and arrange the slices of potato and leek on top.

6 Pour over half of the remaining stock and cook in the oven for 20 minutes until browned.

7 This works great as an accompaniment to any chicken dish.

Rita has always been a keen cook and relished the opportunity to spend time in her kitchen creating some of her favourite dishes. Decorated in a charming cream and green colour, her kitchen has always been her favourite room and time spent here, concocting new dishes, was always a pleasure. This potato and leek bake was a regular meal in her house and as much as she enjoyed making it, her family certainly enjoyed eating it more.

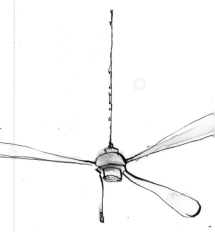

Cod & Beans

by Marie Nolan

INGREDIENTS:

2 x 5oz/ 150g cod fillets, skinned (2 nice thick pieces, centre cut if possible because there are bigger bones)

7oz/ 200g tinned butter beans or cannellini beans, drained

Salt and ground black pepper

7fl oz/ 200ml milk

1 onion, diced

Butter, for frying

1 tbsp cornflour

Serves: 2 / *Preparation time:* 15 minutes / *Cooking time:* 20 minutes

Tip: If you buy cod that is not deboned you can take the bones out of it before cooking by rubbing it with your hands to find the bones and then picking them out with a tweezers.

METHOD:

1 Fry/sauté the onion in a bit of butter until soft, and reserve in a side dish.

2 Bring the milk to a boil and turn down the heat, then poach the cod in the milk until firm, for about 5 minutes.

3 Turn the heat down, remove the poached cod and set aside.

4 Mix a tablespoon of cornflower with a little cold milk into a paste then add this to the cooling milk. Stir or whisk until the milk has thickened.

5 Add the beans and heat the milk mixture, being careful not to allow it to boil.

6 Then add the onion and cod into the sauce.

7 Serve with mashed potatoes and peas or broccoli

Chicken, Rashers & White Wine Sauce

by Delia Tobin

INGREDIENTS:

4 chicken fillets	2oz/50g flour	17fl oz/500ml chicken stock
4 smoked rashers	1 tbsp of white wine	
2oz/50g margarine	1 tbsp of fresh cream	

Serves: 4 / *Preparation time:* 15 minutes / *Cooking time:* 1 hour

METHOD:

1 Preheat the oven to 200°C/400°F/Gas mark 6.

2 Wrap the chicken fillets with the rashers and place in a lightly greased oven-proof dish.

3 Melt the margarine in a saucepan over a medium heat and add the flour to form a roux. Whisk in the stock and white wine and add the cream.

4 Pour the sauce over the chicken, cover with tinfoil and bake in the oven for 30 minutes.

5 Uncover for the last 10 minutes or so to lightly brown.

6 Sprinkle with parsley and serve with roast potatoes and vegetables of your choice.

Tip: Prepare this dish during the day in advance of serving for a relaxed and fuss-free evening meal.

Delia's recipe for Chicken Fillets with Smoked Rashers and White Wine Sauce is a wonderful dinner party recipe as the chicken and sauce can be prepared early on and put in the oven just before your guests arrive

This rich and flavoursome meal can be accompanied by almost any potato or vegetable dish and not only tastes fantastic, but looks great too.

Chicken & Peach Bake

by Mary Healy

INGREDIENTS:

1lb/450g chicken

1lb/450g halved tinned peaches

3oz/75g cheddar cheese, grated

2oz/50g sliced almonds

11oz/300g green beans

WHITE SAUCE:

3oz/75g butter

3oz/75g plain flour

15fl oz/425ml milk

A pinch of freshly grated nutmeg

Salt and pepper

Serves: 4 / *Preparation time:* 30 minutes / *Cooking time:* 40 minutes

METHOD:

1. Preheat the oven to 190°C/375°F/Gas mark 5.

2. Chop the chicken into small pieces, add a small amount of oil to a hot pan and fry until thoroughly cooked and slightly browned on the outside.

3. Arrange the cooked chicken pieces, the beans, the almonds and ¾ of the grated cheese in layers in an ovenproof casserole dish.

4. Next make the white sauce.

5. Gently melt the butter in a saucepan. Add in the flour, salt and pepper.

6. Stir over a low heat with a wooden spoon for a few minutes to let the flour cook.

7. Add a little milk at a time to the flour and butter mix, stirring continuously to remove any lumps until you have a thick creamy sauce.

8. Pour the white sauce over the contents of the casserole dish so it completely covers them and bake in the preheated oven for 20 minutes.

9. After 20 minutes, remove from the oven and arrange the peaches on top, sprinkle with the remaining cheese and bake for a further 10 minutes.

10. Serve with some crisps and salad on the side.

The greatest compliment paid to Mary was that she was the consummate home-maker. She was the heart of the home and family was the most important thing in her life. She was known to all as a wonderful hostess and the ultimate carer and loved to prepare special dishes for her husband, children, grandchildren, and extended family. Mary was an inventive and meticulous cook. She kept records of all her recipes and made sure she never made the same dish twice at dinner parties by keeping a notebook recording what she had served at each and every dinner. A hard-covered manuscript is still in the family kitchen. This treasure contains countless numbers of her recipes, carefully hand-written by her, dating from the 1930s right up to her last entry in 2005. The book is so well used that it is now falling apart. Mary was fascinated by the mysteries and perplexities of domestic fortune, as narrated by Jane Austen and Elizabeth Gaskell and in later years carried a copy of her favourite book Cranford, along with her rosary beads, everywhere she went. Mary knew that good food and good friends were worth far more than an expensive restaurant meal and this recipe was often served for special dinner parties.

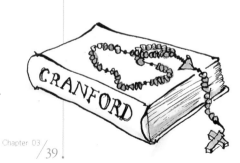

Chicken Curry

by Mona Keane

INGREDIENTS:

4 chicken breast fillets, cut into large pieces

2 large onions, peeled and sliced

3 cloves of garlic, crushed

½ red pepper

½ yellow pepper

Pinch of sugar and salt

3 tbsps curry powder

1 tbsp Chinese five-spice mix

1½ tbsps of cornflour, softened with water

2 pints/1 litre chicken stock

1 bunch fresh coriander leaves, chopped

2 tbsp sunflower oil

Serves: 4 / *Preparation time:* 25 minutes / *Cooking time:* 30 minutes

METHOD:

1 Heat a little sunflower oil in a pan and quickly fry the chicken, until lightly brown. Remove from the pan and leave to one side.

2 Add a little more oil to the pan and sweat the sliced onion, sliced peppers and garlic until soft, but do not let them colour.

3 Add the curry powder and Chinese five-spice mix to the vegetables and cook for a minute or two, then gradually add in the stock.

4 Bring to the boil and skim off any excess fat. If you have used a homemade stock, season to taste with salt and add a pinch of sugar.

5 Thicken slightly with cornflour by adding small amounts, bit by bit, until you have the consistency you like.

6 Now add the chicken to the sauce and simmer for between 6—8 minutes. This will ensure the chicken is cooked through but still moist.

7 Finish the sauce with a tablespoon or two of the chopped coriander leaves. You could also add some reduced fat coconut milk for extra depth of flavour.

Tip: If you leave your curry until the next day, it will always taste much better as all the flavours will fuse together.

Based in the Inner city in Dublin, Mona owned and managed a typical corner grocery shop in the 70s, 80s and 90s. Her customers were true inner city people, as the saying goes; 'the salt of the earth'. Though Mona worked long hours, she always had time for a chat with everyone who came in to the shop. Mona was married to Paud and they had three children; Fiona, Sinéad and Padraig. Sadly, however, her husband died at a young age, leaving Mona to run the business and bring up the children alone. Her children gave her abundant joy and love, which has now expanded to include her five grandchildren. Mona's daughter remembers that her mother always found time to bake; 'as you arrived at our front hall door you were always met with the wonderful smell of baking and looked forward to seeing what delicious treat would be awaiting you.'

After working hard for so long, when Mona retired, she finally had time to do all the things she enjoyed. She attended art classes, and cookery classes. She pursued her interest in fashion and jewellery but most of all she travelled as much as she could, taking in the sights and scenes of far-flung places and experiencing a dizzying array of exciting new tastes; from the USA to Europe, she enjoyed memorable meals in many places.

Smoked Haddock Bake

by Maureen Goggin

INGREDIENTS:

1lb 8oz/700g smoked haddock

2oz/50g mature cheddar cheese

4 hard boiled eggs, peeled and sliced

2 tbsps breadcrumbs

2 tbsps chopped chives or onions

1 onion, sliced

2 bay leaves

Salt and pepper

Paprika

FOR SAUCE

20fl oz/600ml milk
to poach fish

2oz/50g butter

2oz/50g plain flour

2 tbsp cream

Tip: If the smoked fish flavour is too strong, use half smoked haddock and half unsmoked fish

Serves: 4 / *Preparation time:* 40 minutes / *Cooking time:* 20 minutes

METHOD:

1 Preheat the oven to 190°C/3575°F/Gas mark 5.

2 Cut the haddock into small pieces and poach by placing in the milk with the bay leaves, season with salt and pepper and simmer on a low heat for 10 minutes. Take off the heat and allow to cool. Retain the milk for the sauce.

3 Flake the fish and layer the sliced eggs and fish in an ovenproof dish.

4 Sauté the onion with the butter and add the flour. Stir well.

5 Remove from the heat and stir in the retained milk used to poach the fish. Heat again until thick.

6 Add the chives to the sauce and mix well, then pour it over the fish and eggs.

7 Top the dish with the cheese and breadcrumbs and a little paprika.

8 Bake for about 15—20 minutes in the oven until golden brown and the cheese is bubbling.

Chicken & Broccoli Bake

by Mary Healy

INGREDIENTS:

4 chicken breasts

1lb/450g broccoli

2oz/50g breadcrumbs

2oz/50g grated cheese

5fl oz/150ml cream

5fl oz/150ml mayonnaise

5fl oz/150ml chicken stock

3 tsp mild curry paste

1 large tin of cream of chicken soup

Salt and pepper

1tsp chopped parsley to garnish

This is a great dish to serve when you have guests as it can be assembled well in advance and just needs to be popped in the oven when your guests arrive, leaving you free to enjoy their company.

Serves: 4 / *Preparation time:* 15 minutes / *Cooking time:* 1 hour

METHOD:

1 Preheat the oven to 180°C/350°F/Gas mark 4.

2 Cut the chicken breasts into bite sized pieces and cook on a hot pan in a little oil until gently browned.

3 Cut the broccoli into small florets and add to a boiling saucepan of water to simmer for about 3—4 minutes.

4 Layer the chicken and the broccoli in an ovenproof casserole dish.

5 Mix the soup, cream, mayonnaise and curry paste together with the prepared stock and season well.

6 Pour the creamy mixture over the chicken and sprinkle with a mixture of the grated cheese and breadcrumbs.

7 Bake for 50—60 minutes and serve with boiled new potatoes coated in a little butter and sprinkled with parsley.

Luigi's Family Pasta Sauce

by Luigi Rea

Ingredients:

1lb/450g minced beef

1lb/450g steak pieces

4 cloves of garlic, peeled and chopped

3 tins of chopped tomatoes

1 glass of red wine

4 tbsp olive oil

1 tube of tomato puree

Salt

Sprigs of basil and thyme (optional)

Serves: 6—8 / *Preparation time:* 15 minutes / *Cooking time:* 2 hours

Method:

1 Cover the base of a large saucepan with a layer of olive oil and add the garlic, mince and steak. Fry on a high heat until the meat has changed colour then add the tomato puree and continue to fry until the oil turns a deep red colour.

2 Add the wine and chopped tomatoes and continue to stir until it comes to the boil. Add salt to taste.

3 Turn the heat down low, add the herbs and continue to simmer very slowly for at least 2 hours. The longer you leave it to simmer, the richer the sauce will taste. If you feel the sauce is getting too dry add a small cup of water.

4 Serve with pasta and crunchy white bread.

Though this recipe is as Italian as they come its creator, Luigi, has always laughingly referred to himself as 'more Irish than the Irish themselves'. As a young man Luigi enlisted in the Irish army and served the country for two years during the Emergency, some of the most difficult days in Irish history. A natural aptitude for mending machinery, a genius for tinkering and a logical and rational mind made him a valuable addition to the national service. As a young boy he had specialized in mending clocks, learning by taking them apart and putting them back together again until he understood their workings and he developed his knowledge in the army.

Though a determinedly hard worker Luigi always had time for family and friends and is known as a sociable and outgoing person. That typical Italian passion for spending time with family and sharing mealtimes together is exemplified by Luigi who loved to cook for his children and made, what is now known as, 'Luigi's Family Pasta Sauce' as often as it was requested. Indeed, Luigi could have been in a spaghetti ad himself, with his black curly hair, classic Italian features and wide beaming smile, always on the brink of laughter. The only problem with this dish, his wife Julia notes, is that as it cooks, it decreases in volume, as clandestine mouthfuls are sampled along the way!

Fish Cobbler

by Maura Scanlon

Ingredients:

1lb/450g white fish, e.g. haddock or cod

7oz/200g plain flour, (or 100g plain and 100g wholemeal)

2oz/50g margarine

2oz/50g of grated cheddar

4 fl oz/100ml milk

1 tsp baking powder

A pinch of salt

Cheese sauce:

2oz/50g margarine

2oz/50g flour

2oz/50g grated cheese

17fl oz/500ml milk, heated

1 egg yolk

Salt and pepper to taste

Serves: 4 / *Preparation time:* 1 hour / *Cooking time:* 40 minutes

Method:

1 Preheat the oven to 200°C/400°F/Gas mark 6.

2 Steam the fish until cooked.

3 Make the scone base. Sieve the flour, baking powder and salt into a bowl and rub in the margarine to resemble bread-crumbs. Add the grated cheese to the mix and make a well in the centre. Gradually add the milk to the dry ingredients and mix in from the sides until all the milk is used and the mixture resembles a soft dough.

4 Knead the dough gently on a floured surface and cut out as many round scones as you can with a cutter or cup.

5 Next, make the cheese sauce by melting the margarine in a saucepan on a medium to high heat and adding the flour to form a roux. Slowly whisk in the heated milk then add in the cheese and egg yolk, on a lower heat, whisking all the time.

6 To assemble the cobbler, flake the steamed fish and place into an ovenproof dish.

7 Pour the cheese sauce over the fish and place the cut out scones on top.

8 Sprinkle some grated cheese over the entire dish and bake in the oven for 30—40 minutes, or until golden brown.

Maura's husband Joseph, and his father Joseph, were both residents of Our Lady's Hospice. Joseph only found out in later years that his father had been cared for in the same place where he was and this gave him great comfort.

Maura first met Joseph at the Duke Street Skating Rink, next to the Crystal Ballroom. She would cycle for ages to get from Cabra, via Berkeley Road, to go skating, a hobby she adored. She had her skates constructed specially for her by a shoemaker and they hung from her bicycle handles as she powered through the city on her way to the rink. The day she met Joseph she knew her life was about to be transformed; romance blossomed as they spun along to the music and she fell in love. They married and had three children and had a wonderful life together.

Since her husband Joseph passed away Maura is stoic about being a widow. Her children and neighbours are a source of constant joy and consolation. She has a phrase for the (rare) days when she does not talk to anyone, she calls it her 'shut mouth day'. She knows just what to do; she prepares a delicious, comforting meal for one, relishes every bite and then sits down and calls a friend or two.

Chapter 04

Irish Originals

o/o/o

Original Irish Stew

by Sister Catherine Horan

INGREDIENTS:

1lb 2oz/500g diced lamb	14oz/400g diced potatoes	2 carrots
2 tbsp barley	2 onions	2 tbsp chopped parsley
		1 beef stock cube

Serves: 4 / *Preparation time:* 15 minutes / *Cooking time:* 2 hours

METHOD:

1 Place the lamb in a saucepan, cover with water and bring to the boil.

2 Add in the stock cube and simmer for 45 minutes to an hour.

3 Add in the vegetables, potatoes and barley. Simmer for a further 30 minutes, until the lamb and vegetables are tender. The barley should thicken the sauce.

4 Season to taste and garnish with chopped parsley.

Sister Catherine grew up on the South Circular Road and her memories centre around the heart of her childhood home; the kitchen. 'My mother was a fantastic chef and cooked on a rusty old gas stove. Her dishes were tastier than a five star hotel's. The tiny kitchenette that these great meals emerged from was little to behold. It was old fashioned and basic. In those days there were no fridges or washing machines, no luxuries. To light the oven you had to put your head into the gas stove!'

Sister Catherine affectionately recalls that when her mother made this stew, which was on their family menu, twice a month, she used no specific quantities. She just had it down pat; a spoon of barley here, a fist of flour there, throw in a stock cube... The potatoes were always cooked separately but discretion was used when it came to vegetables as the family had an allotment near Drimnagh so had seasonal access to fresh onions, carrots, marrows, peas, potatoes and herbs. The resulting stew was always a delicious treat. This recipe is dedicated to the memory of Sister Catherine's mother.

Nettle Soup

Sister Margaret Madden

INGREDIENTS:

8oz/225g young nettle leaves

1oz/25g butter

3 medium potatoes, peeled and chopped

1 large onion, peeled and chopped

1 pint/600ml milk (you can substitute cream for part of this if you like)

1 pint/600ml vegetable or chicken stock

Bunch of tied herbs – rosemary, sage, thyme, mint

Serves: 6 / *Preparation time:* 10 minutes / *Cooking time:* 20 minutes

Sister Margaret used to pick nettles for soup every spring. Nettle soup goes back centuries and is a traditional Irish soup that many older people remember from their childhoods. The best time to pick nettles is April and the nettles are good until May. Her top tip is to always wear gloves!

METHOD:

1 Melt the butter in a saucepan, add the chopped potatoes and onions, season with salt and pepper, cover and sweat by cooking on a gentle heat for 8—10 minutes, stirring every now and then.

2 Add the stock and the milk and bring to the boil. Reduce the temperature and allow the liquid to simmer until the potatoes are cooked.

3 Add the nettles and herbs and boil uncovered until the nettles are wilted. Do not overcook as the soup will lose its fresh green colour and flavour.

4 Remove the herbs and then puree the soup. Taste the soup and add some salt and/ or pepper if necessary.

5 Serve with wheaten soda bread and butter.

Tip: Spinach, kale or watercress may be replaced for all or some of the nettles in this recipe.

Tea Brack

by Agnes Southwell

INGREDIENTS:

10oz/275g flour

8oz/225g sultanas

8oz/225g raisins

5oz/150g brown sugar

2oz/50g melted butter

1 large cup of cold tea

2 large eggs

Pinch of salt

1 tsp baking powder

Small tub of cherries and some candied peel

Chopped nuts if desired (e.g. almonds, walnuts)

Serves: 6—8 / *Preparation time:* 15 minutes / *Cooking time:* 1 ½ hour

Agnes' Tea Brack was always a firm favourite of her husband Hugh and her daughters Marie and Sylvia.

METHOD:

1 Preheat the oven to 190°C/375°F/Gas mark 5.

2 Place all the dried fruit into the cold tea and leave to steep somewhere cool overnight.

3 The next day, take the bowl of tea-soaked fruit and add the remaining ingredients, mixing well as you add each ingredient.

4 Grease and line a 2lb loaf tin and pour the mixture in.

5 Bake for approximately 1 ½ hours until a skewer or knife comes out dry from the centre of the loaf.

6 Leave to cool before serving with butter.

Dublin Coddle

by Mary Doyle

INGREDIENTS:

1lb/450g pork sausages

1lb/450g bacon rashers, chopped into small pieces

5 carrots

1 vegetable stock cube

5 medium potatoes (floury type is best, e.g. Queens)

1 large or 2 medium onions, sliced

Pinch of mixed herbs

Pepper to taste

Barley and other vegetables can be added if desired

Serves: 6—8 / *Preparation time:* 20 minutes / *Cooking time:* 2 hours

This recipe for coddle comes from Mary's own childhood. She grew up on it and it is one of her favourites. She's in good company too as it is said to have been a favourite dish of Jonathan Swift, Dean of St. Patrick's Cathedral and author of Gulliver's Travels.

METHOD:

1 Peel and cut the potatoes and onions in half.

2 Scrub the carrots and dice them.

3 Put the meat, potatoes and vegetables, pepper, stock cube, and herbs into a large saucepan and cover over with water.

4 Bring to the boil, then reduce the temperature and allow to simmer for about 2 hours, until the meat is cooked. Alternatively you can cook it in the oven at a low temperature for 3 hours.

5 Leave to cool slightly or leave overnight as this allows the flavours to combine.

—o/o/o—

Gur Cake

by Mary Doyle

INGREDIENTS:

8 slices of stale bread, brack or other cake

6oz/175g currants or mixed dried fruit

4oz/110g granulated sugar

3oz/75g plain flour

3oz/75g mixed peel

2oz/50g butter, melted

3 eggs
(2 for the mix and 1 for the glaze)

5fl oz/150ml cold tea

2 tsps mixed spice

Pinch of salt

FOR THE PASTRY:

½ tsp baking powder

8oz/225g plain flour

4oz/110g butter

½ tsp salt

Serves: 8—10 / *Preparation time:* 30 minutes / *Cooking time:* 1 hour

1 Preheat the oven to 190°C/375°F/Gas mark 5.

2 Make the shortcrust pasty first by mixing together the plain flour, salt and butter in a large mixing bowl. Using your fingertips, rub the butter into the flour until it resembles fine breadcrumbs.

3 Mix in 2—3 tablespoons of cold water and knead the mixture lightly to form a firm dough. Wrap the dough in Clingfilm and place in the refrigerator for 30 minutes.

4 Remove all the crusts from the bread and cut or break into crumbs or small pieces. Put this into a mixing bowl with the flour, salt, baking powder, mixed spice, sugar and dried fruit.

5 Mix well to combine and add the butter and 2 eggs with enough tea to make a fairly stiff mixture.

6 Grease an 11 X 7 X 2 inch (28 X 18 X 4cm) tin. Take the pastry out of the fridge and roll out to ½ cm thick using the baking pan/tin as a guide. Cut out two large pieces of pastry to act as the base and top of your cake and line the tin with one of the pieces of pastry from edge to edge.

7 Spread the pastry base with the cake mixture and place the second sheet of pasty over the top. Pat gently, prick with a fork and glaze with eggwash. Sprinkle some sugar over the top.

8 Bake in the oven for 50—60 minutes, until golden and leave to cool in the tin before cutting into slices.

An experienced cook, Mary worked as professional confectioner and baker for Gateaux for most of her life and loved her job. Even with nine children and a full time job, Mary was adept at coming up with new ideas for cakes and baked goods for her family too and she enjoyed creating innovative new designs and decorations for them. Long before cake transfers were even invented Mary figured out a way to design a cake with a hologram of a £20 note. She had a passion for art and would have loved to have been an artist of some type but is philosophical about life and where her decisions have taken her, commenting that 'opportunities come and go, how does one know which decision is the right one?' However, her optimism and confidence in her own life choices is obvious when she says laughingly; 'If you say you can, you're right; if you say you can't, you're right'.

Gur cake was an invention of Dublin bakers in the 1930s as a way to use up day-old bread or cake. The name 'Gur' comes from an old Irish slang word for children who did not attend school regularly. 'To go on the Gur' was a common phrase for not attending school and Gur cake may well have got its name from being a favourite cheap snack for a kid out on the street for the day. It was always the cheapest thing in the bakery, usually a penny a slice, and can still be bought in some modern bakeries or supermarkets, now named 'Fruit Slice'.

Queen of Puddings

by Kate Davis

Ingredients:

3oz/75g sugar

2oz/50g breadcrumbs

15fl oz/425ml milk, warmed

2 eggs

Jam, any flavour you like

Serves: 2 / *Preparation time:* 20 minutes / *Cooking time:* 70 minutes

Method:

1 Preheat the oven to 200°C/400°F/Gas mark 6.

2 Put the breadcrumbs, egg yolks and ⅓ of the sugar into a mixing bowl and beat well. Add the warmed milk and mix thoroughly. This forms the base of the pudding.

3 Spread a little jam over the base of a pie dish or ovenproof dish (approx 14 x 16cm) and add the mixture on top, spreading evenly.

4 Place in the oven for about 45 minutes to bake.

5 While the base of the pudding is baking, make the meringue mixture by whisking the 2 egg whites until stiff and adding the rest of the sugar until a creamy, thick meringue texture is achieved.

6 Remove the base of the pudding from the oven and spread a little jam over it before piling on the meringue.

7 Return to the oven for a further 20—25 minutes until the top of the meringue is lightly coloured.

8 Serve hot with ice cream.

Kate was brought up with a Nanny, who she dearly loved. She remembers being five or six years old, sitting at her table in the nursery, her little legs swinging from the edge of the chair in anticipation as she eagerly awaited her serving of this dessert. She vividly recalls the white oblong dish with the blue stripe around the side that Queen of Puddings was always served in.

Just thinking about this dish brings back the sense of excitement she felt as a little girl as she watched while her nanny cut through the gooey meringue topping of her favourite pudding. This is a childhood favourite of Kate's that brings back happy memories. We hope you will enjoy it as much as she did.

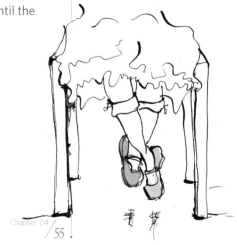

Potato Cakes

by Winifred Greene

Ingredients:

1lb/450g cold mashed potato

1oz/25g butter, melted

1 tbsp chopped parsley

Salt & pepper

1 tbsp sieved flour

Serves: 2—3 / *Preparation time:* 10 minutes / *Cooking time:* 10 minutes

Method:

1 Put all the ingredients into a bowl and mix together. Turn out onto a floured board and roll out to about ½ inch thick using a rolling pin dusted with flour to avoid sticking.

2 Using a round cutter or cup, cut out as many cakes as you can.

3 Fry in a hot pan, lightly greased, with oil or butter, for 2 minutes on each side. Alternatively you can grill the cakes on both sides.

4 When cooked serve them warm with butter.

Winnie's small kitchen, where she cooked these potato cakes on cold winter days, was always occupied by two helpful assistants; Packie and Susie, her cats. The walls of the kitchen were primrose yellow. The front door was bright pink and was always open to friends and neighbours. Her husband Henry removed a wall between the hall and the kitchen to allow for a counter and table so the family could fit comfortably together. He took a great interest in making her centre of operations bright and functional because he loved her food and the sense of security he found in the most important room in the house.

On the television, Winnie's daughter recalls, the Waltons seemed to be always on. Pat Kenny on the radio sobered her up – she loved current affairs - but the best sound of all was the sound of her children laughing. This recipe was handed down from Winnie's mother and her daughters continue to cook her recipes.

Tip: You can use left-over mashed potato for these. Put the potato in a bowl, cover it and pop it in the fridge to be used the next day. Cyprus potatoes or King Edwards work best.

Colcannon

by June & Daniel Fincher

Ingredients:

3lb/1.35kg potatoes	2oz/50g butter	Small bunch of spring onions
6fl oz/175ml milk	1 head curly kale	Salt & ground black pepper

Serves: 6—8 / *Preparation time:* 20 minutes / *Cooking time:* 1 hour

Method:

1 Peel and quarter the potatoes and simmer in lightly salted water until they are cooked.

2 While the potatoes are cooking, wash the curly kale, remove the core and chop the leaves. Boil the kale in a little salted water for a few minutes until soft. If you don't have curly kale you can use dark green leafy cabbage instead.

3 Chop the spring onions, half roughly and half finely. Add the roughly chopped spring onions to the drained kale and place in a food processor. Pulse for about 10 seconds. When kale is cooked it shrinks and is difficult to separate so will be lumpy if not shredded in the food processor.

4 When the potatoes are just cooked, put the milk in a pan and bring to the boil. Drain the potatoes and add half the butter. Mash the potatoes while still warm and slowly add enough boiled milk until the potatoes are fluffy. Add the curly kale and finely chopped spring onions to the potatoes. Add salt and pepper for seasoning.

5 Place the colcannon into a serving dish. Colcannon is a delicious teatime meal served with a fried egg on top. It is also a tasty lunch served with sausages or gammon.

Tip: Colcannon can be prepared ahead of time and kept in the fridge. To reheat, place a knob of butter on top, cover with tin foil, and reheat in a moderate oven, 180°F/350°F/Gas mark 4 for 20—25 minutes.

Mealtimes are times not to be messed with for Daniel. His wife, June, claims you could set your clock by him; lunch at 1pm, tea at 6pm and supper at 9pm. Family mealtimes were an important part of the daily routine and the table had to be set properly; good cutlery and napkins laid out neatly, an elegant table for a hearty meal. Daniel always looked after the preparation of the tea, that was his responsibility, and he would take it very seriously. He would bring in perfectly made ham, egg and cheese sandwiches to be enjoyed by the fire and big mugs of tea, three sugars in his, to satisfy his sweet tooth. In fact, Daniel's sweet tooth was something their children inherited too. June used to bake fairy cakes with butter icing for the family but always had to ice them covertly and quickly lest the children came in, eager for a preview tasting! In the Fincher household, Fridays were 'Cook Days' when lots of the weekly cooking was accomplished and Daniel was the self-appointed chief taster! In those days, the menu was very much traditional Dublin fare, like coddle, tripe and colcannon, the recipe brought to you here.

Chapter 05

Perfect Puddings, Tarts & Pies

o/o/o

Bread and Butter Pudding

by Mary Murray

Ingredients:

3 slices white bread	½ oz/15g sultanas	1 egg
2oz/50g butter	15fl oz/425ml milk	Nutmeg
1oz/25g caster sugar		

Serves: 1—2 / *Preparation time:* 15 minutes / *Cooking time:* 45 minutes

Method:

1 Preheat the oven to 200°C/400°F/Gas mark 6.

2 Cut the bread into fingers, butter it and place into a greased small ovenproof dish, approximately 16 x 14cm, in layers, with sultanas sprinkled between each layer, until the dish is ¾ full.

3 Heat the milk in a heavy bottomed saucepan and stir in the sugar until it is dissolved. Beat the egg and pour the heated milk onto it taking care it does not curdle.

4 Pour this mixture over the bread in the dish and grate a little nutmeg on top.

5 Place the dish on a flat tin and bake in the oven for about 45 minutes until quite set and nicely brown.

6 Sift a little icing sugar on top and serve at once.

Mary's mother used to bake this simple recipe for bread and butter pudding for all her children, albeit with adjusted quantities to cater for all 10 of her offspring! Mary has continued on with the family tradition by cooking it for her niece who used to call in after school most days to enjoy a dish of it. This is a simple and easy recipe that can be effortlessly tailored to individual tastes and occasions by the addition of things like chocolate, nuts or fruit. According to Mary it's as enjoyable to make as it is to eat.

Apple Sponge Pudding

by Mairéad and Christy Reid

INGREDIENTS:

1lb 8oz/700g cooking apples

6oz/175g flour

4oz/110g butter or margarine

4oz/110g caster sugar

3oz/75g sugar

½ tsp cinnamon

1 egg, beaten

½ tsp of baking powder

A few drops of vanilla essence

Serves: 4—6 / *Preparation time:* 20 minutes / *Cooking time:* 50 minutes

METHOD:

1 Preheat the oven to 180°C/350°F/Gas mark 4.

2 Peel and slice the apples thinly and place in layers in a large pie dish, with a sprinkle of sugar and cinnamon between each layer. Top with one last layer of apple slices (don't sprinkle sugar on this last layer).

3 Beat the margarine and caster sugar to a smooth cream and add in the egg.

4 Mix in the flour and baking powder, add a few drops of vanilla essence, and beat thoroughly. The mixture should be quite stiff. However if it becomes too stiff add a drop of milk to thin it out.

5 Spread the sponge mixture over the apples so they are completely covered and cook for approximately 40 minutes on the top shelf of the oven.

6 After 40 minutes cover with two layers of greaseproof paper and continue to cook for 10 more minutes.

7 When the sponge is cooked it will be slightly firm to the touch.

8 Serve with hot custard or cold ice cream. Slices of the pudding can be frozen individually for use as needed.

Tip: This dish works equally well with rhubarb or fresh or tinned peaches.

Mairéad and Christy made this Apple Sponge Pudding nearly every week for 50 years. A favourite with their family, it quickly moved up the recipe list until it was top of the menu. Working seamlessly together, Mairéad and Christy would bake this for Sunday dessert; he peeling the apples and she slicing them, together conjuring up a delightful dessert. Though they cooked in harmony, their views on how their favourite desert should be served differed; hot custard was perfect according to Christy, cold ice cream ideal according to Mairéad... why not try both?

o/o/o

Easy Sherry Trifle

by Delia Tobin

Ingredients:

1 jam Swiss roll	1 apple	1 tin mandarin segments
2 bananas	1 pear	1 measure of sherry
1 packet of strawberry or raspberry jelly	1 pint/600ml ready made custard	Fresh cream to decorate

Serves: 6—8 / *Preparation time:* 20 minutes / *Cooking time:* 2—3 hours

Method:

1 Make up the jelly by dissolving the block of jelly in 10fl oz/300ml hot water and topping up with the same quantity again of cold water (or as per instructions on packet). Add the juice from the mandarins and stir well.

2 Line the bottom of a large bowl or dish with the Swiss roll and pour over the measure of sherry. You can add slightly more than one measure if preferred.

3 Slice the fruit thinly and layer it, along with the mandarin slices, over the sponge.

4 Pour the jelly mixture over the fruit and cover. Leave to set in the fridge for 2—3 hours.

5 When set, pour over the custard (ensure it is cool) and pipe fresh whipped cream on the top. Serve immediately.

Delia ran a large Bed & Breakfast in Limerick for many years and so catering for large numbers was an everyday occurrence in her home. Perhaps because of all the cooking she did there, her kitchen became one of her favourite places, the sound of the electric mixer a regular soundtrack to the usual household sounds of children playing, guests moving about, and people chatting by the fire. Every day Delia would rustle up six brown cakes and dozens of scones with the greatest of ease. Guests never went hungry in Delia's home. This recipe for Sherry Trifle is such a simple and easy one and it always got the thumbs up from family and guests alike.

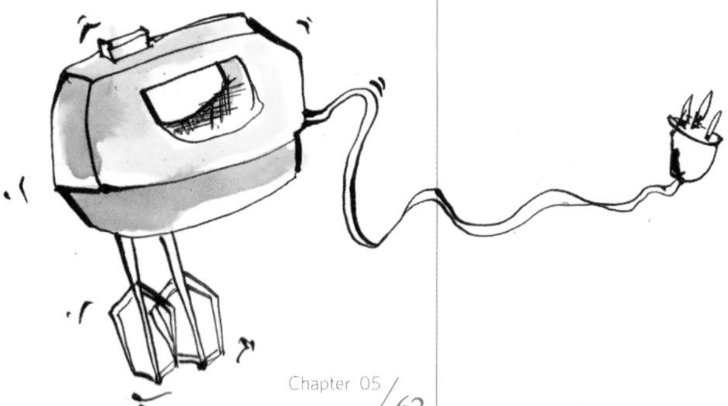

Pavlova Log

by Mona Garvey

INGREDIENTS:

5 egg whites	½ tsp vinegar	10fl oz/300ml cream
10oz/275g caster sugar	Couple of drops of vanilla essence	Whipped cream and fruit to fill
½ tsp cornflour		

Serves: 6—8 / *Preparation time:* 40 minutes / *Cooking time:* 40 minutes

Mona, along with her best friend Mary, throws parties at which she loves to serve her much anticipated pavlova; crammed full of fresh fruit and cream, with a sticky, gooey centre, it's utterly irresistible.

METHOD:

1 Preheat the oven to 150°C/300°F/Gas mark 2.

2 Beat the egg whites until stiff with an electric whisk and add in the sugar gradually, beating all the time. When you have added all the sugar, add in the cornflour, vinegar and vanilla essence and gently fold it all in together.

3 Prepare a long sandwich or Swiss roll tin, approx 12 inch x 9 inch (30 x 22cm), and lay parchment or baking paper across the base.

4 Spread the meringue mixture evenly across the lined tin with a spatula or flat knife.

5 Cook in the oven for 30 minutes.

6 Remove from the oven and leave to cool.

7 When cool, spread whipped cream and your choice of fruit across the pavlova without going right to the edges. Using the parchment paper, roll the pavlova up loosely, don't worry if it cracks as you go, just pat it into place and keep going.

8 Serve in slices with some fresh fruit on the side.

Lemon Curd Meringue Tarts

by June & Daniel Fincher

INGREDIENTS:

6oz/175g plain flour

3oz/75g margarine

2oz/50g caster sugar

¼ tsp baking powder

1 large egg yolk

3 tbsp of milk to mix

LEMON CURD FILLING:

4fl oz/150ml water

4oz/110g caster sugar

1oz/25g cornflour

1oz/25g butter

1 egg yolk

Juice and rind of 1 lemon

MERINGUE:

3oz/75g caster sugar

1 egg white

These Lemon Curd Meringue Tarts were always one of Daniel's favourite tea-time treats.

Makes: 20 Tarts / *Preparation time:* 1 hour / *Cooking time:* 30 minutes

METHOD:

1 Preheat the oven to 180°C/350°F/Gas mark 4.

2 To make the pastry sieve the flour and baking powder into a bowl, add in the caster sugar and then rub in the margarine.

3 Whisk one egg yolk with the milk, make a well in the centre of the dry ingredients, and pour into the centre. Mix from the outside in until a soft dough is achieved. Wrap the pastry in Clingfilm and place in the fridge for about 15 minutes.

4 To make the lemon curd filling, boil the water and add the sugar, lemon juice and zest. Thicken with the cornflour and once the right consistency is arrived at remove from the heat.

5 Next, add the butter and whisk in the egg yolk. Leave to cool and move on to making the meringue topping.

6 Whisk the sugar into the egg whites until the mixture forms stiff peaks.

7 To assemble the tarts, grease a tray of shallow, mini tartlet tins. Roll the pastry out thinly and individually line each hollow with a matching amount of pastry. Place a good teaspoon of lemon curd on top of the pastry. Cover with a tablespoon of the meringue and bake for 30 minutes, covering with greaseproof paper after 20 minutes.

8 When cooked, remove from the tins and serve individually with a mint leaf on top.

Our Apple Tart

by Joe Connolly

INGREDIENTS:

1lb/450g self-raising flour	8oz/225g white sugar	Pinch of salt
8oz/225g margarine	3 large cooking apples	1 cup of cold water

Serves: 6 / *Preparation time:* 25 minutes / *Cooking time:* 45—50minutes

METHOD:

1 Preheat the oven to 180°C/350°F/Gas mark 4.

2 Put the flour and salt into a large bowl. Add the margarine in small pieces. Rub both together well until they have the consistency of breadcrumbs.

3 Add the water slowly and bind it all together, using your hands, into a doughy mixture.

4 Break off one big piece of the dough, approximately ¾, and cut into 2 even pieces on a board dusted liberally with flour. You can keep the remaining dough wrapped in Clingfilm in the fridge or freezer for another occasion or use it to create decoration for the top of the tart.

5 Roll out one piece of the dough using flour to stop it sticking and place it as the base of your pie into a greased and floured 9 inch (23cm) pie tin.

6 Slice the apples and layer into the tin over the dough. Sprinkle liberally with the sugar.

7 Roll out the other piece of dough and gently place over the apples, sealing the edges around the tin.

8 Cut and trim the excess dough from around the rim and add scallops or pleats using your thumb by pressing gently at intervals around the edge.

9 Place the tart into the preheated oven, on the middle shelf, and bake for approx 45—50 minutes or until golden brown.

10 For the happy taste of childhood serve the warm apple tart with heated custard.

The family get-together happened every Sunday when Joe's wife Kay's parents would arrive for dinner, mostly for conversation because, as Kay recalls, Joe was not much of a cook, though he was always willing to try! He would read the recipe first, quite methodically and then get on with the weighing which he called 'the weighside experience'. Eventually, he got to know how far into the bowl to pour the flour and that became his new method of 'weighing' ingredients. He used to roll out the pastry with a milk bottle, leave it to cool in the fridge and the family would head off to mass.

Those days money was scarce and extravagance an unknown word.. The only sweet thing their four boys ever got was 'Our Apple Tart', and they loved it.

Joe and Kay became practised at making them and soon they were making them for everyone, from the Ladies Club to the Church Cake Sale committee. On a Saturday, they would bake 20 apple tarts, scalloped around the edges, pleated and sugared on top, stacking them up the stairs like an assembly line, right up to the landing. Memories are baked into these pies.

Apricot Trifle & Homemade Custard

by Loretta Roddy

TRIFLE INGREDIENTS:

1 jam Swiss roll

1 packet of lemon or orange jelly, made to instructions

1 tin of apricots

2fl oz/50ml sherry

10fl oz/300ml cream, to decorate

CUSTARD:

2 eggs

10fl oz/300ml milk

I tsp sugar

A pinch of nutmeg

Serves: 6—8 / *Preparation time:* 30 minutes / *Cooking time:* 4—5 hours

Loretta's daughter, Marguerite's, most vivid childhood recollection of her mother is of watching her standing at the kitchen counter, next to the cream Rayburn stove, wearing her bright yellow and baby blue apron, as she writes recipes into her dog-eared cookery journal.

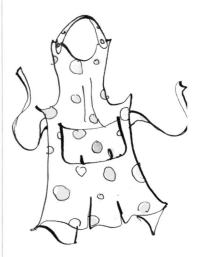

METHOD:

1 Cut up the Swiss roll into chunks and place in a large presentation bowl, patting down to create the base of your trifle.

2 Pour the sherry and the juice from the tin of apricots over the Swiss roll pieces and allow to soak in. Layer the apricots across the base.

3 Make up the jelly according to the packet instructions and pour over the fruit.

4 Place in the fridge to set and in the meantime get on with making the custard.

5 Put a pan of water to boil on the stove. In a separate bowl or jug beat the eggs with the milk, sugar and nutmeg. When combined, place this into the hot water to heat through, stirring all the while, the custard will begin to cook. When the custard is thick enough to coat the back of the spoon it is ready.

6 Allow the jelly on your trifle to set for 2—3 hours then pour the cooled custard over and leave to set for a further 2 hours in the fridge before serving.

7 Decorate with whipped cream and a sprinkle of nutmeg.

Rhubarb Crumble

by Winifred Greene

INGREDIENTS:

1lb/450g rhubarb	3oz/75g caster sugar	1oz/25g porridge oats
7oz/200g brown/ Demerara sugar	2oz/50g softened butter	1 tsp ground cinnamon
	2oz/50g flaked almonds	A pinch of salt
4oz/110g plain flour		

Serves: 4—6 / *Preparation time:* 25 minutes / *Cooking time:* 45 minutes

METHOD:

1 Preheat the oven to 180°C/350°F/Gas mark 4.

2 Prepare the rhubarb by cutting it into 1 inch pieces. Wash it and then put it into a deep saucepan with the cinnamon, brown sugar and 3 tbsp of cold water. Cover and cook for 5 minutes, simmering over a low heat, until the rhubarb is soft.

3 To make the crumble, sieve the flour into a bowl, add the salt and mix. Add the softened butter and, using your fingers, work the butter through the flour until it has the consistency of breadcrumbs.

4 Add the porridge oats, half the flaked almonds and the caster sugar and mix well.

5 When the rhubarb is cooked, transfer it to an ovenproof dish and sprinkle the crumble mixture over it evenly.

6 Sprinkle the remaining almonds over the top and bake for about 45 minutes or until the crumble is a golden brown colour.

7 Serve with custard, fresh cream or ice-cream.

Tip: If you are reheating this later, an extra sprinkle of cinnamon will bring the crumble back to life.

The combination of tartness and sweetness in this classic crumble makes it a firm favourite of Winifred's and one she always sought second helpings of as a child. When she went on to make it for her own children, they participated in the preparation by gathering and cutting the rhubarb, fresh from the garden. Nowadays most of us buy rhubarb from supermarkets.

Chapter 06

Afternoon Tea

ofofo

Oxford Lunch

by Margaret (Mari) Cullen

INGREDIENTS:

12oz/ 350g plain flour, sieved

8oz/225g margarine (at room temperature)

8oz/225g caster sugar

4oz/110g cherries, washed, dried and halved

4oz/110g mixed peel

1oz/25g ground almonds

1lb 8oz/700g sultanas

5 eggs

Juice of 1 orange

Serves: 8—10 / *Preparation time:* 30 minutes / *Cooking time:* 3 ½ hours

METHOD:

1 Preheat the oven to 150°C/300°F/Gas mark 2.

2 Prepare a deep 9 inch (23cm) round or 8 inch (20cm) square cake tin by greasing it and lining it with greaseproof paper.

3 Place the margarine and sugar into a large mixing bowl and cream together with a wooden spoon.

4 Add the eggs to the bowl and mix, followed by the flour and almonds, again mixing until all the ingredients are fully incorporated.

5 Add the juice of the orange and the fruit and mix again.

6 Place the mixture into the prepared tin and using the back of the wooden spoon, smooth over the top.

7 Bake in the pre heated oven, on the middle shelf, for 3—3½ hours approximately. You can test when it's ready by piercing the centre with a skewer and if it comes out clean it's cooked.

8 Allow the cake to cool in the tin. When cold, turn it out of the tin and remove the greaseproof paper.

9 Wrap the cake in double greaseproof paper and again in foil and it can be stored well in an airtight tin, perfect for when unexpected guests drop around!

Tip: Mari always felt that electric mixers produce dry cakes so if you do use a mixer use the slow button and finish off the final mix in a bowl with a wooden spoon.

Mari liked plain straight-forward cooking and when baking she liked 'the old reliables', such as coffee cake, sponges, scones, oxford lunches, apple tarts and rich Christmas cake with homemade almond icing.

As a housewife, with a busy home to run, Mari's fail safe recipes were those that were nourishing, did not need a plethora of ingredients and did not take too long to prepare.

Scotch Pancakes

by Seán O'Riain

INGREDIENTS:

14oz/400g plain white flour   ½ tsp salt   2 eggs, well beaten

4oz/110g sugar   1 level tsp bread soda   ½ pint Buttermilk

Serves: 24 pancakes / *Preparation time:* 10 minutes / *Cooking time:* 20 minutes

These scotch pancakes are the perfect accompaniment for afternoon tea.

METHOD:

1. Sieve the flour into a bowl and add the sugar, salt and bread soda. Mix well together.

2. Stir in the beaten eggs and some buttermilk with a wooden spoon and continue to mix. Keep adding the buttermilk until you get the right consistency. You want to make a nice dropping mixture, the texture should be not too runny, but thick enough to coat the spoon. Allow to stand for half an hour or more.

3. After it's been left to stand, beat the mixture thoroughly again. Heat a non-stick heavy duty pan until quite hot and oil it a very small amount just to prevent any sticking.

4. Drop on spoonfuls of the mixture in small round circles. When the pancakes start to show bubbles, turn over with a spatula and cook the other side.

5. Place the cooked pancakes onto a tray and keep warm.

6. These are delicious served with jam and cream.

Tip: A handy tip to test if your pan is hot enough is to drop a blob of cold water onto the pan, if it runs in little balls, it is the right heat.

Cherry Loaf

by Margaret (Mari) Cullen

INGREDIENTS:

8oz/225g plain
flour, sieved

6oz/175g margarine,
at room temperature

6oz/175g caster sugar

4oz/110g glacé
cherries, washed,

dried and quartered

1oz/25g ground almonds
optional

3 eggs, beaten

¼ level tsp
baking powder

DECORATION:

2oz/50g glacé cherries,
washed, dried and
halved for the top

2 heaped tbsps apricot
jam, boiled and sieved
to glaze

*Mari's food philosophy is simple;
the best ingredients and a simple
recipe make the tastiest meal and
the happiest family.*

Serves: 6—8 / *Preparation time:* 20 minutes / *Cooking time:* 1 hour

METHOD:

1 Preheat the oven to 160°C/325°F/Gas mark 3.

2 Cream the margarine and the sugar together until pale
and smooth.

3 To this mix add the eggs, sieved flour and baking powder,
stir well.

4 Add the cherries and the almonds and gently fold in.

5 Place the entire mix into a greased and lined 2lb/900g loaf tin
and bake for 1 hour on the middle shelf of the oven.

6 Check it is ready by inserting a skewer or knife into the centre
of the cake, if it comes out clean then it is cooked.

7 Leave it in the tin until it is cool and then turn it out and
remove the greaseproof paper. Brush with the boiled apricot
jam for a glaze and sprinkle the glacé cherries on top.

Mills Inn Porter Cake

— by Kathleen Kelly —

Ingredients:

1lb/450g sultanas

1lb/450g flour

8oz/225g butter

8oz/225g brown sugar

4fl oz/120mls Guinness

4oz/110g glacé cherries, chopped

4oz/ 110g mixed peel, chopped

3 eggs, beaten

1 tsp mixed spice

½ tsp salt

¼ tsp baking soda

Grated rind of 1 lemon

Serves: 6—8 / *Preparation time:* 20 minutes / *Cooking time:* 2 hours

Method:

1 Preheat the oven to 180°C/350°F/Gas mark 4.

2 Grease and line an 8 inch (20cm) cake tin.

3 In a mixing bowl, cream together the butter and sugar until smooth and add the beaten eggs, a little at a time, alternating with the flour.

4 Add the Guinness and mix well.

5 Add the salt, baking soda, spices, lemon rind, and fruit and mix well.

6 Pour the batter into the prepared tin and bake for about 2 hours.

7 Allow to cool slightly before turning onto a wire rack to cool the rest of the way through.

Kathleen has two large scrapbooks of recipes she has collected over the years and finds it hard to select a favourite. Having always found great pleasure in baking for her loved ones, food and her family life were inextricably intertwined and each recipe holds a particular personal memory for her.

She always loved sitting on the kitchen steps in the sunshine with a cup of tea, in that peaceful space before the hustle of dinner. She would take time out to mediate in her lively garden, with a mug of tea and Smokey the cat for company before returning to the heart of her home where delicious concoctions like this rich porter cake were created. The kitchen has always been a place of joy, where everyday her family came together to laugh and talk, and eat home-cooked food with pleasure and happiness.

Fruit Sponge

by Margaret McCormack

Ingredients:

7oz/200g plain flour

5oz/150g caster sugar

2oz/50g sultanas

5oz/150g margarine, melted

1 tsp baking powder, sieved

3 eggs

3fl oz/75ml milk

Serves: 4—6 / *Preparation time:* 20 minutes / *Cooking time:* 50 minutes

Method:

1 Preheat the oven to 180°C/350°F/Gas mark 4.

2 Beat together the margarine and sugar until light and creamy.

3 Gradually add in the flour, baking powder and the eggs, a little at a time.

4 When the mix is fully blended, add in the fruit. You can add any dried fruit to this recipe to suit your taste but sultanas are particularly nice.

5 Pour the cake mix into a greased and lined 2lb loaf tin and bake for approximately 50 minutes.

6 Test that the cake is ready by inserting a skewer into the centre of it, if it comes out clean it's fully cooked.

7 Turn out and leave to cool on a wire tray.

8 Serve with cream and jam.

A proud Tipperary woman, Margaret enjoys her television, especially cheering on her home team in the hurling matches. When she's not supporting her blue and gold team she's often found searching out her favourite colours in the garden. Once the bright yellow daffodils started to appear that was her cue that spring was on its way and there would be lots of sunshine and fresh air to enjoy.

Margaret knows our Lady's Hospice like the back of her hand because she used to work in the kitchens of the Hospice for many years before she became a resident. Margaret enjoys baking and her absolute favourite is this Fruit Sponge, a deliciously simple and quick moist cake that will have a queue lined up at the kitchen door once the smell starts to waft out of the oven. A cup of tea and a slice of this tasty cake in the garden on a summer evening is undeniably lovely.

Carrot & Sultana Scones

by Maureen Goggin

INGREDIENTS:

8oz/225g plain flour	2fl oz/50ml milk	Pinch of nutmeg
2oz/50g margarine	1 tbsp sugar	Pinch of salt
2oz/50g sultanas	1 beaten egg, to glaze	
1 medium carrot, grated	1 tsp baking powder	

Makes: 8 / *Preparation time:* 20 minutes / *Cooking time:* 25 minutes

METHOD:

1 Preheat the oven to 200°C/400°F/Gas mark 6.

2 Mix the flour, salt and baking powder in a bowl and rub in the margarine until it takes on the consistency of fine breadcrumbs.

3 Stir in the rest of the ingredients and make into a soft dough. Knead it well with a little flour.

4 Roll out the dough to ¼ inch thick and cut into squares or circles (you can use a glass dipped in a little flour for this). Brush the tops lightly with the beaten egg to give them a golden colour when they cook.

5 Bake for 20—25 minutes until golden brown and enjoy.

Maureen was always a busy woman and along with caring for her family she was also an astute business woman. Attached to her house in Caherciveen was her shop which sold everything one could imagine; from a needle to an anchor, from animal food to wool for knitting, and lots more besides. In those days ingredients and groceries were measured out by hand and so Maureen would carefully sell loose tea by the kilo and weigh out brown sugar into paper bags for baking, all the while chatting to her customers and learning more about cooking and baking as each person came through the doors. Inventive, creative and experimental with food, this recipe for Carrot and Sultana Scones came about when she was making a batch one afternoon and decided to see what they would taste like with the addition of some leftover grated carrot. They were a sure-fire hit and she's been making them ever since.

Banana Loaf

by Agnes Southwell

INGREDIENTS:

8oz/225g
self-raising flour

2oz/ 50g chopped nuts
(pecans and walnuts
work best)

6oz/175g brown sugar

3oz/75g margarine

4 bananas

3 eggs

½ tsp salt

Dried fruit, as desired

Serves: 6—8 / *Preparation time:* 15 minutes / *Cooking time:* 1 hour

This Banana loaf was Agnes's favourite. Agnes baked every single day so that her children would arrive home from school to the delicious warm scent of a fresh treat as soon as they opened the front door.

METHOD:

1 Preheat the oven to 180°C/350°F/Gas mark 4.

2 Beat together the margarine and sugar until pale and creamy.

3 Add the eggs, a little at a time, and then gently beat in the flour and salt.

4 Mash the bananas. Add the bananas, fruit and nuts to the mix and gently fold in.

5 Place the mixture in a lined tin and bake for 1 hour.

6 This is delicious served slightly warm with butter.

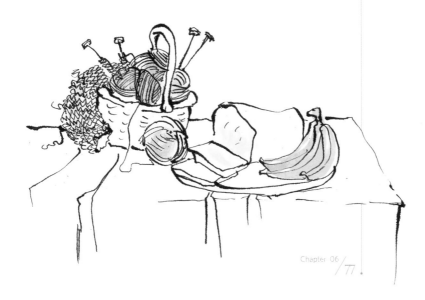

Fruit Scones

by Ethel Woodful

INGREDIENTS:

1lb 5oz/600g plain flour	4oz/110g caster sugar	3 eggs
4 ½oz/125g butter	9fl oz/275ml milk	½ tsp salt
4 ½oz/125g sultanas	2 level tsp bread soda	

Makes: 10 / *Preparation time:* 25 minutes / *Cooking time:* 20 minutes

METHOD:

1. Preheat the oven to 180°C/350°F/Gas mark 4.

2. Sieve the flour and baking powder into a bowl.

3. Cut the butter into pieces and rub it into the flour until it resembles bread crumbs.

4. Add the caster sugar and sultanas to the mix and stir.

5. Make a well in the centre of the dry ingredients and add the milk and 2 beaten eggs. Mix thoroughly until you have a soft dough, you can add more milk if the consistency is too dry.

6. Turn the dough onto a floured board and knead lightly. Roll out to approximately 1 - 1 ½ inches thickness and brush the top with 1 beaten egg.

7. Cut out scone shapes and bake on a greased or lined baking tray in the oven for 15 - 20 minutes.

8. Serve warm with cream and jam.

Determined, confident and with a can-do attitude, the hallmark of Ethel's character has always been that nothing can stand in her way. At a time when women were not expected to take financial matters into their own hands, Ethel single-handedly negotiated and obtained a loan from the bank and bought a property, something unheard of in the days when men were the decisions makers and the only decisions a woman could make were in the kitchen.

Yet for all her determination and strong-mindedness, Ethel's great love was caring for and nurturing her family. With six strapping boys to feed cooking was undertaken with military precision. Planning ahead was a necessity and Ethel would bake dozens of scones, brown bread and buns each weekend to last the week, though the boys ensured that they never did. A strategically planned menu meant preparing meals was hassle free; roast beef on Sundays, leftovers on Mondays, Steak and Kidney pie on Tuesdays, Wednesdays was corned beef and cabbage (her boys' favourite) and on Thursdays the fisherman's van came by and her sons might bring home up to twenty mackerel which saw them through till Sunday. Funnily enough, Fridays was coincidentally the day the family cat, Sergeant, reported to the kitchen for duty...

Apricot Surprise Swiss Roll

by Kathleen Barker

INGREDIENTS:

4oz/110g flour	1 tsp baking powder	Pinch of salt.
4oz/110g sugar	Pinch of cinnamon	Cream to decorate
4 eggs	Tin of apricots	Fresh apricots to serve

Serves: 4—6 / *Preparation time:* 20 minutes / *Cooking time:* 20 minutes

Kathleen, or Kay as she prefers to be called, is known for being such a good cook that her neighbour once actually prayed she would make this dessert for her! This is an unusual and yummy take on the traditional Swiss role. You won't be able to resist a second slice.

METHOD:

1 Preheat the oven to 180°C/350°F/Gas mark 4.

2 Whisk the sugar and eggs until light and fluffy and fold in the flour. Add a pinch of cinnamon, salt, 1 teaspoon of baking powder and mix together.

3 Grease and line a Swiss roll tin (approx 25 x 35 cm). Smooth the mixture into it evenly and bake for 20 minutes.

4 When cool, spread good quality raspberry or apricot jam over the entire surface and roll the sponge up. Leave the roll on a wire rack to fully cool before cutting into slices.

5 Serve with fresh whipped cream and fresh apricots.

Chapter 07

Charming Cakes

o/o/o

Chocolate Cake

by Margaret Linnane

INGREDIENTS:

6oz/175g self-raising flour

1oz/25g of cocoa powder

4oz/110g plain chocolate, broken in pieces

6oz/175g butter

6oz/175g caster sugar

4 eggs, separated

2 tbsp milk

1 tsp vanilla essence

CHOCOLATE ICING:

6oz/175g icing sugar

3oz/75g caster sugar

1oz/25g of cocoa powder

1 ½ oz/40g butter

2 tbsp water

Serves: 6—8 / *Preparation time:* 40 minutes / *Cooking time:* 40 minutes

METHOD:

1 Preheat the oven to 180°C/350°F/Gas mark 4.

2 Cream the butter, sugar and vanilla essence together until smooth.

3 Melt the chocolate slowly in a bowl over a pan of hot water then beat the melted chocolate into the creamed butter and sugar. Beat in the egg yolks and the milk.

4 Sift the flour and the cocoa powder into the mixture and fold in.

5 Whisk the egg whites in a separate bowl and gently fold into the mixture.

6 Divide the mixture evenly between two greased 8 inch (20cm) circular tins and bake in oven for 20—25 minutes. When they are cooked, turn them out and leave to cool on a wire rack.

7 To make the icing, melt the butter, caster sugar and water in a saucepan on a low heat, stir continuously and do not let it boil. Pour this onto the sieved icing sugar and cocoa powder and mix well until smooth. Leave sit for ten minutes.

8 Spread half the icing over one of the cakes and layer the other cake on top. Use the rest of the icing to spread over the top.

9 Serve with fresh cream or ice cream.

10 Leave to sit for 10 minutes.

Margaret's daughter, Virginia's, childhood memories are woven around the taste of this rich chocolate cake. Her mother used to make it for her and her classmates at the Holy Child Convent every Friday without fail. Once the girls reached sixth year in school they had their own private common room where they would convene in peace for afternoon breaks to savour the delicious treat. Virginia became so sentimental about this significant childhood ritual that she in turn passed it on to her own children, making the exact same cake for her boys whilst they were at school. The recipe has passed on, like all good recipes should, through the ranks of the family. The best recipes should be shared and the Linnane family hope you and yours enjoy this chocolate cake just as much as they have.

Tip: For extra rich icing, add 1oz melted chocolate and 1 tbsp water to the icing ingredients.

Prune & Walnut Cake

by Kathleen Kelly

INGREDIENTS:

12oz/350g wholemeal flour

6oz/175g prunes, chopped

4oz/110g light muscavado sugar

3oz/75g margarine

4oz/110g walnuts, chopped

2 tsp baking powder

2 tsp cream of tartare

1½ tsp cinnamon

1 egg

4fl oz/125ml semi-skimmed milk

Serves: 6—8 / *Preparation time:* 20 minutes / *Cooking time:* 45 minutes

METHOD:

1 Preheat the oven to 180°C/350°F/Gas mark 4.

2 Mix together the flour, baking soda, cream of tartare and cinnamon.

3 Rub in the margarine with your fingertips until it resembles the consistency of breadcrumbs.

4 Stir in the prunes, sugar and walnuts.

5 Beat the eggs and milk into the mixture, pour into a 2lb (900g) loaf tin and bake in the oven for 45 minutes.

6 When ready, leave to cool in the tin before turning out.

7 Slice, serve and enjoy with a cup of tea.

When she ran a busy home and family, Kathleen used to love sitting on the steps of the house enjoying a slice of this cake with a cup of tea, taking some precious time out to savour life before the hustle continued.

Rhubarb & Orange Sponge

by Kathleen Kelly

Ingredients:

1lb/ 450g rhubarb

2 bananas, sliced

1—2oz/25—50g sugar, or to taste

Grated rind of half an orange

Juice of 1 orange

3oz/ 75g fine wholemeal flour

2oz/50g self-raising flour

1 level tsp baking powder

4oz/110g butter or margarine (at room temperature)

4oz/110g soft brown or caster sugar

2 large eggs

Serves: 6—8 / *Preparation time:* 20 minutes / *Cooking time:* 45 minutes

Method:

1 Preheat the oven to 190°C/375°F/Gas mark 5.

2 Trim the rhubarb, wash it and cut it into small pieces.

3 Grease a shallow ovenproof dish and put the rhubarb into it with the sliced bananas. Sprinkle the sugar, orange juice and grated rind over it.

4 Mix together the wholemeal flour, self-raising flour and baking powder in a bowl. Put the soft butter or margarine into a separate bowl and beat it a little to make it workable, then add the sugar, eggs and the flour mixture to it and mix everything together well to make a soft, but not sloppy, mixture. If it is too stiff, adjust the consistency with a little milk. Drop this mixture in small spoonfuls over the rhubarb. Spread it evenly if you can but don't worry as it will spread out during cooking.

5 Bake in the preheated oven, just above the centre, for 35—45 minutes until the fruit is tender and the sponge is golden and cooked through. Test with a knife or skewer which will come out clean when the sponge is cooked.

6 Serve with crème fraiche or yoghurt.

Tip: For a variation on this recipe use sliced cooking apples, such as Bramleys, instead of the rhubarb (omit the bananas). In autumn try using blackberries, or a mixture of blackberries and apples.

I used to go to Mackey's Garden Centre, Henry Street in March and buy half a dozen rhubarb plants, called Red Champagne, for this recipe. These are very sweet and tasty. In April, rhubarb sticks used to cost up to 50 cents each in a supermarket but an investment of about €4.00 per plant yielded an abundant harvest for five years! I planted them in the top garden and by June they were fully grown but you can only cook them the next year as they get stringy by August. The leaves are poisonous but good for the compost heap.

On my way to the rhubarb patch I used to love to stop for a cup of tea in the sunshine. Any Abba song always brings this time back to me! But never for long! I would think of my family and hurry on up to the patch to collect the rhubarb for the cake. You cannot cut rhubarb instead you must pull off the stalks gently and leave an inch or so behind. Wash them. Cut them diagonally in one or two inch pieces into a bowl, rinse them and you're ready to go. Follow my directions faithfully and your family will plead with you to bake this dessert every day.

Coffee Cake

by Margaret (Mari) Cullen

INGREDIENTS:

6 oz/175g margarine
(at room temperature)

6 oz/175g caster sugar

3 large eggs

6oz/175g self-raising
flour, sieved

1 tbsp coffee essence

COFFEE ICING:

3oz/75g margarine
(at room temperature)

8 oz/225g icing sugar,
sieved

1 tbsp coffee essence

1 tbsp milk

Alice, Mari's mother, liked this cake.

Serves: 6—8 / *Preparation time:* 20 minutes / *Cooking time:* 25—35 minutes

METHOD:

1 Preheat the oven to 180°C/350°F/Gas mark 4.

2 Prepare two 6 ½ or 7 ½ inch sandwich tins (16 or 19cm)
  by greasing and lining them with greaseproof paper.

3 Put all the ingredients into a mixing bowl and beat with
  a wooden spoon until well mixed (2—3 minutes).

4 Place half of the mixture in each of the prepared tins.

5 Bake on the middle shelf in the preheated oven for 25—35
  minutes. When cooked, turn out and remove the papers,
  leave to cool on a wire tray.

6 To make the icing, put all the ingredients into a mixing bowl
  and beat well with a wooden spoon until smooth.

7 Sandwich the two cakes together with half of the icing and
  pipe the remaining icing onto the top of the cake.

o/o/o

Sinful Pineapple Layered Cake

by Noeleen O'Connor

INGREDIENTS:

1 pint of cream, whipped

1 tin of pineapple pieces or one fresh pineapple cut into chunks

1 tsp of baking powder

1 tin of crushed pineapple

4oz/110g flour

4oz/110g sugar

4 eggs

Fresh, delicious, sweet and sticky; this cake is a really sinful indulgence!

Serves: 6—8 / *Preparation time:* 30 minutes / *Cooking time:* 20 minutes

METHOD:

1 Preheat the oven to 180°C/350°F/Gas mark 4.

2 Grease and line two Swiss roll tins, approx 20 X 30cm.

3 Cream the eggs and sugar together until pale and smooth.

4 Sieve the flour and baking powder and fold into the egg and sugar mixture.

5 Pour the mixture into the two tins and shake gently to settle. Place in the oven on the middle shelf for 20 minutes or until golden.

6 When cooked, take them out of the oven and leave to rest for 2 minutes before turning out onto a wire tray and leaving to fully cool with a tea towel covering them.

7 Meanwhile drain the crushed pineapple and mix it into the whipped cream.

8 Drain the pineapple pieces and set aside the juice.

9 With a large bread knife, slice through each of the sponges to make two cakes so that you know have 4 layers. Remove the crust or any rough edges.

10 Place one sponge on to a large serving plate and drizzle some pineapple juice over it. Spread some of the pineapple cream over the surface and dot with pineapple pieces.

11 Place the next sponge on top and repeat the layering process.

12 When all 4 layers are completed spread the remaining pineapple cream over the top and sprinkle with chocolate flake.

13 Cut and serve.

Crazy Cake

by Etta Kearney

INGREDIENTS:

5oz/150g raisins, soaked overnight in sherry or any other drink of choice

10oz/275g butter

1 packet of digestive biscuits

8oz/225g milk chocolate

1—2 tbsp cocoa powder

1 tbsp golden syrup

2oz/50g whole nuts or almonds

Serves: 6—8 / *Preparation time:* 20 minutes / *Cooking time:* 3—4 hours

This take on chocolate biscuit cake is so called because when Etta used to make it she would add whatever she had in her cupboards to it; from marshmallows to sweets and from broken biscuits to glace cherries, you can make this as crazy as you like!

METHOD:

1 Melt the butter, chocolate, golden syrup and cocoa powder together in a bowl over a saucepan of hot water on a medium heat.

2 Crush the biscuits until they are just slightly larger than breadcrumb-sized.

3 Combine everything together, add anything else you'd like to add at this stage, and place the mix into a greased and lined loaf tin.

4 Leave to set in the fridge for 3-4 hours before removing it from the tin.

5 Slice into wedges to serve.

Tip: Some suggestions to add to this cake are; mini marshmallows, rice krispies, crushed pecan nuts, maltesers, chocolate drops or dried fruit.

Golden Christmas Cake

by Patricia Flynn

INGREDIENTS:

4oz/110g crystallized pineapple or dried apricots

4oz/110g glacé cherries

4oz/110g walnuts

6oz/175g butter

6oz/175g caster sugar

12oz/350g sultanas or raisins

9oz/250g self-raising flour

3 large eggs

2-3 tbsp sherry

½ level tsp salt

ALMOND ICING:

1lb/450g ground almonds

8oz/225g caster sugar

8oz/225g icing sugar

2 tsp of whiskey

Serves: 12—16 / *Preparation time:* 45 minutes / *Cooking time:* 2—2½ hours

METHOD:

1 Preheat the oven to 170°C/325°F/Gas mark 3.

2 Grease and line an 8 inch (20cm) cake tin, round or square is fine.

3 Rinse the pineapple and cherries in warm water to remove the sugar, then pat dry and chop (if you are using apricots you don't need to rinse them). Put the fruit into a basin with the walnuts and sultanas or raisins and mix well.

4 Sift the flour and salt into a separate bowl and set aside.

5 Cream the butter and sugar together until light and fluffy. Into this, beat the eggs and gradually beat spoonfuls of the flour mixture into this. When well mixed fold in the rest of the flour alternately with the sherry.

6 Add the fruit and nuts and mix very well. Turn the mixture into the tin and level off by tapping the base against a hard surface.

7 Put into the centre of the oven, covered lightly with greaseproof paper, and bake for one hour. Lower the heat to 150°C/300°F/Gas mark 2 and bake for a further 1½—2 hours.

8 Cool in the tin for 20 minutes then turn out onto a rack.

9 To make the icing mix all the ingredients together in a bowl, adding 1 tbsp of water to bind together until it resembles the texture of pastry dough.

10 Roll out with a small bit of flour to prevent sticking and cover the cold cake completely in icing before you are ready to serve it.

Patricia Flynn loved her fashion and always liked to be smart, recalls her daughter, Mo. A spirited person with a great sense of humour. She was very intelligent, though from a family where university was not considered for girls, a huge frustration for her. Patricia read widely and she became a top class bridge player, establishing the first bridge club in Mullingar. She loved her Irish Times crossword.

Patricia was an excellent cook, but not interested in being tied to the kitchen and you certainly would never have seen her in an apron. Her Christmas cake recipe was inherited from her mother but she actually recorded six different Christmas cake recipes in her personal recipe book. In her house the kitchen had a tilted floor so, of course, every year the cake would come out of the oven slanted! For Patricia's children, slicing the top off the cake to make it even was a really special part of the Christmas preparations - a delicious preview of what was to come on Christmas day. This is a popular favourite which can be made in early December as it is not so rich.

Welsh Cake

—— by Catherine (Kay) Craddock ——

INGREDIENTS:

9oz/250g flour

4 ½oz/125g margarine, cut into pieces

5 fl oz/150ml cold water

A pinch of salt

FOR THE SPONGE

5oz/150g sugar

5oz/150g margarine

3 eggs

5oz/150g flour

Jam, any flavour to sandwich the layers together

Serves: 8—10 / *Preparation time:* 30 minutes / *Cooking time:* 30 minutes

METHOD:

1 Preheat the oven to 200°C/400°F/Gas mark 6.

2 Make up a shortcrust pastry base by rubbing the margarine pieces into the flour until it resembles the consistency of breadcrumbs, adding the salt, and then combining it all together with the cold water.

3 Knead the pastry gently on a floured surface and wrap in Clingfilm. Place in the fridge while you make the sponge.

4 Prepare the sponge layer by beating together the flour, eggs, butter and sugar with a wooden spoon.

5 Take your pastry out of the fridge and roll out to approximately 25 X 35cm. Place into a greased and lined Swiss roll tin or shallow ovenproof dish and spread your preferred flavour jam across the surface. Pour the sponge mixture on top and bake in the oven for approximately 20—25 minutes, until cooked through and lightly golden brown on the top.

6 When the cake has cooled, cut into slices and serve with whipped cream.

Kay lives along the Grand Canal in Dublin in a brownstone house with black turrets and friendly windows which look out on to the passing swans as they go about their business. On a typical day you will find Kay at her kitchen table with a cup of tea and a good book, possibly a Maeve Binchy, munching on a slice of Welsh Cake. As she looks out the window at her graceful feathered neighbours she is always reminded of Yeats' poem, The Wild Swans of Coole. *Sometimes, the simplest pleasures combine themselves into the most rewarding of moments, and are all the more precious for their effortlessness.*

This recipe for Welsh Cake was passed down from Kay's mother-in-law, Mrs. Craddock. Though there is a traditional 'Welsh Cake', usually a type of scone made with raisins, this cake is not of the same family. In fact, it is a bit of a mystery why this particular cake was christened 'Welsh Cake' as the origin of the name has been lost in its history but amongst Kay's family and friends, this is the only type of 'Welsh Cake' worth eating!

Yoghurt Cake

by Margaret O'Toole

INGREDIENTS:

1lb/450g of sultanas

1 x 125g carton of yoghurt (orange is best but you can try out other flavours)

2 x yoghurt carton measurements of caster sugar

1 yoghurt carton of sunflower oil

3 x yoghurt carton measurements of self-raising flour

3 eggs

Serves: 6—8 / *Preparation time:* 10 minutes / *Cooking time:* 1 ½ hours

This unique cake is so fresh and light and perfect on a summer's day. You can use the yoghurt carton to measure out the other ingredients making it really quick and easy to prepare. This recipe came from Margaret's sister Maureen Maguire.

METHOD:

1 Preheat the oven to 200°C/400°F/Gas mark 6.

2 Mix all the ingredients together thoroughly with a wooden spoon.

3 Line a 7 inch (18cm) round baking tin and pour the cake mixture in. Tap the base of the tin to let it settle evenly.

4 Put into the oven for between 1¼ and 1½ hours.

5 After 1¼ hours check if it is done by piercing the centre with a knife or skewer, if it comes out clean, it's cooked. It may need another 15 minutes.

6 Serve with a dollop of natural yoghurt and a sprig of mint.

Chapter 08

Cookies & Buns

—o/o/o—

Peanut Butter Cookies
(Gluten Free)

by Mary Groves

Ingredients:

7oz/200g rice flour (gluten-free flour, available in most large supermarkets)

7oz/200g brown sugar

5oz/150g butter

5oz/150g peanut butter

1 egg

1 tsp baking powder

Makes: 12—15 / *Preparation time:* 10 minutes / *Cooking time:* 15—20 minutes

Method:

1 Preheat the oven to 180°C/350°F/Gas mark 4.

2 Cream together the butter and the sugar until pale and smooth and then beat in the peanut butter and egg.

3 When the mixture is well beaten and smooth, sieve in the baking powder and rice flour and mix well.

4 Lightly oil a baking tray and place spoonfuls of the mix on the tray, ensuring you leave space between each one for the cookies to expand.

5 Bake in a preheated oven for 15—20 minutes until lightly golden.

6 Remove from the tray and leave to cool on a wire rack.

Tip: For an extra treat add some chocolate chips to the mix.

Mary's vision of her perfect moment is sitting by the window in a red brick house, enjoying her favourite peanut butter cookies and a cup of tea, listening to Lyric fm and looking out the window. She has always wanted to own a house in the West of Ireland and her idea of it is clear in her mind. It would be near a cliff top, so you can see both the waves crashing against the rocks and the clouds scudding across the blue sky. It would have a slanted roof and curtains at the windows which are Georgian blue and white gingham. She would sit at the window looking out across the cliffs at the seagulls as they swoop and soar, their noisy chatter keeping her company.

Sometimes, this is what great recipes can do for a person; transport them to a special place.

Coconut Buns

by Sister Catherine Horan

Ingredients:

8oz/225g flour

3oz/75g butter
or margarine

3oz/75g sugar

4 fl oz/150ml of milk

2oz/50g
desiccated coconut

1 tsp baking powder

1 egg, beaten

Pinch of salt

To decorate:

Jam
(any flavour you like)

Desiccated Coconut

 Makes: 12 buns / *Preparation time:* 15 minutes / *Cooking time:* 20 minutes

Method:

1 Preheat the oven to 200°C/400°F/Gas mark 6.

2 Sieve the flour, baking powder and salt into a bowl.

3 Rub in the butter, then add the sugar and the coconut
   and mix well.

4 Add in the egg and half the milk and mix well to a fairly stiff
   consistency, you can add more milk if you need to.

5 Take tablespoonfuls of the mixture and place into paper bun
   cases. Continue until all the mixture is used.

6 Bake in the oven on a baking tray for about 20 minutes.

7 When ready, remove them from the tray and leave to cool.

8 Brush with a little warm jam and dip in the coconut to finish.

Coconut Slices

by Íde Ó Háinle

INGREDIENTS:

6oz/175g caster sugar

3oz/75g desiccated coconut

3 egg whites

1 packet short-crust pastry

4—5 tbsp raspberry jam

Ide's unique recipe for Coconut Slices is a big favourite with her own family. Combining gooey meringue and flaky sweet pasty it's a scrumptious dessert that's sure to impress.

Serves: 8—10 / *Preparation time:* 20 minutes / *Cooking time:* 30 minutes

METHOD:

1 Preheat oven to 170°C/325°F/Gas mark 3.

2 Roll out one sheet of the short crustpastry, place on a lined Swiss roll tin (approx 35 X 25cm) and cover with the raspberry jam.

3 Make the meringue topping by beating together the 3 egg whites with an electric mixer and adding in the caster sugar, little by little, as you beat them until you have formed a creamy mixture that forms peaks. Stir in the coconut.

4 Smooth the meringue topping over the pastry base, dredge lightly with caster sugar and bake in the oven for 30 minutes or until the meringue topping has turned a light golden colour on the peaks.

5 Remove from the oven and leave to cool for a few minutes before serving in slices.

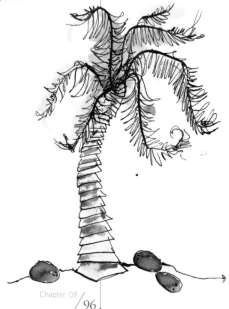

Hidden Treasure Treats

—— by Noeleen O'Connor ——

Ingredients:

4 x 100g Dairy Milk
chocolate bars

9oz/250g Rice Krispies

1 bag (approx 250g)
of 'fun size' chocolate
treats of your choice

(Noeleen suggests
Mars, Twix, Maltesers,
Crunchie… but whatever
takes your fancy!)

Serves: 6—8 / *Preparation time:* 10 minutes / *Cooking time:* 2 hours to set

These fun store-cupboard treats can be made different every time, depending on what you find in your kitchen presses. They are an exciting version of rice krispie treats that kids will love, especially as they never know exactly what is in them, and will have fun guessing!

Method:

1 Melt the chocolate in a bowl over a pot of hot water.

2 Pour the Rice Krispies into a big mixing bowl.

3 Break up the treasure (the mini treats) and add to the Rice Krispies.

4 Pour the melted chocolate over and mix well.

5 Turn into a Clingfilm lined tin (approx 35 x 25 x 6cm) and chill for a few hours until set.

6 Slice carefully and watch out for the treasure!

Tip: Other treasure you can experiment with could include: raisins, marshmallows, Skittles, white chocolate drops, nuts, popping candy or broken cookies, you can be as creative as you like.

Mint Slices

by Íde Ó Háinle

INGREDIENTS:

7oz/200g butter

4oz/110g caster sugar

2 x 100g bars
of mint chocolate
(Cadbury's mint
crisp is ideal)

3 tbsp drinking
chocolate powder

1 large egg, beaten

2 x packets of polo
biscuits, crushed

CHOCOLATE TOPPING

1 x 100g bar of
dark chocolate
(70-85% cocoa
content is best)

1 capful of peppermint
essence

Serves: 8—10 / *Preparation time:* 10 minutes / *Cooking time:* 2 hours

METHOD:

1 Melt the caster sugar, butter, mint chocolate and the drinking chocolate powder in a saucepan on a low to medium heat.

2 Add the beaten egg and the 2 packets of crushed biscuits and mix well.

3 Press the mixture into a lined Swiss roll tin (approx 35 x 25cm).

4 Next, melt the bar of cooking chocolate and add the peppermint essence to it.

5 Stir and smooth on top of the chocolate biscuit base.

6 Leave to set in the fridge for 2 hours before slicing into small sized bars.

Tip: You can store these for a few days in a tin.

Oatmeal Cookies

by Mary Healy

INGREDIENTS:

6oz/175g oatmeal	6oz/175g margarine	1½ tbsp Golden Syrup
6oz/175g plain flour	2oz/50g caster sugar	¾ tbsp bread soda

Makes: 16 / *Preparation time:* 15 minutes / *Cooking time:* 15—20 minutes

METHOD:

1 Preheat the oven to 160°C/325°F/Gas mark 3.

2 Mix the oatmeal, flour and sugar together in a large bowl.

3 Melt the margarine and golden syrup slowly together and add to the dry ingredients, mix well.

4 Press the mixture into a Swiss Roll tin (approx 35 x 25cm) and bake in the oven for 15 minutes or until golden brown.

5 Mark and cut into squares while hot and still in the tin. Leave in tin to cool before removing.

The greatest compliment paid to Mary was that she was the consummate home-maker. She was the heart of the home, the guiding light and a safe harbour. Family was the most important feature in her life and hospitality to all was her sacred mission. This recipe for Oatmeal cookies was one of her most frequently used recipes. She always had a tin of these cookies on hand for the children, and later the grandchildren, to enjoy. Sometimes, the simplest acts, like offering homemade oatmeal cookies to a friend or family member, can be the most rewarding.

o/o/o

Fruit Slices

by Christine Sullivan

INGREDIENTS:

7oz/200g
ready-made puff pastry

7oz/200g stewed apple

1 tbsp caster sugar

1 tbsp sultanas and raisins
(steeped in hot water
overnight and strained)

1 egg, beaten

Pinch of mixed spice

Whipped Cream

Serves: 6 / *Preparation time:* 20 minutes / *Cooking time:* 15—20 minutes

METHOD:

1 Preheat the oven to 220°C/425°F/Gas mark 7.

2 Roll out the pastry to around 2mm thick, cut into 6 even-sized
rectangles and place on a greased baking sheet. Pierce with a
fork all over, brush with the beaten egg and bake for 15—20
minutes. Allow to cool.

3 Mix the stewed apple with the sugar, fruit and mixed spice.

4 Cut each of the cooked pastry rectangles in half horizontally.

5 Distribute the apple mix over the 6 bottom halves of pastry
and spread evenly. Top with a layer of freshly whipped cream
and place the top halves of the pastry on each slice.

6 Dust with icing sugar to serve.

Chapter 09

Entertaining Friends

–o/o/o–

— o/o/o —

Whiskey Punch

— by Patricia Flynn —

Ingredients:

Boiling water	3 cloves	1 measure of
2½ tsp brown sugar	1 slice of lemon	Irish Whiskey (Jameson preferably)

Serves: 1 / *Preparation time:* 5 minutes

Method:

1 Heat a glass by rinsing it with warm water.

2 Stud the slice of lemon with the cloves.

3 Dissolve the sugar in a little boiling water, keep the metal spoon in the glass to prevent cracking.

4 Add the whiskey, studded lemon slice and fill up with boiling water. Enjoy.

Patricia enjoyed a hot whiskey punch both for therapeutic reasons as well as purely for enjoyment. She suffered from bad circulation and when it was very cold in Mullingar she would drink this in a real punch glass, inherited from her father. She was particular that an order of business be followed: the lemon had to be studded with cloves, the glass had to be warmed, and it had to have a spoon inside, to prevent the glass from cracking. This is truly a recipe to be followed!

Marilyn Monroe Chicken

by Noeleen O'Connor

INGREDIENTS:

4 chicken breasts, boneless and skinless

1 medium onion, finely chopped

14oz/400g mushrooms, roughly chopped

8 ½ fl oz/250ml fresh light cream

1 measure of brandy

1oz/25g butter

1 tbsp olive oil

Salt and pepper

This recipe is so called because it includes brandy, apparently Marilyn's tipple of choice!

Serves: 4 / *Preparation time:* 15 minutes / *Cooking time:* 25 minutes

METHOD:

1 Preheat the oven to 200°C/400°F/Gas mark 6.

2 Tenderise the chicken breasts by bashing them with a rolling pin.

3 Coat them with olive oil and sprinkle with salt and pepper.

4 Heat a griddle pan to a high temperature and sear the chicken on both sides.

5 Place in an oven dish and finish cooking in the oven for 25 minutes until cooked through. Reserve the juices for the sauce.

6 Meanwhile, sauté the onions in butter in a saucepan on a medium heat until soft and golden.

7 Add the mushrooms and continue to cook for another 3 minutes.

8 Add the brandy and bring to a rolling boil. Cook off the alcohol.

9 Add the cream and reserved juices from the chicken and reduce to a pouring sauce.

10 Pour over the chicken and serve with baby potatoes and green beans.

Paratha

(Layered Bread)

by Eileen D'Cruz

Ingredients:

6oz/175g sieved
wholemeal flour

6oz/175g plain flour

7fl oz/200ml water

5fl oz/150ml vegetable
oil or melted ghee

½ tsp salt

Serves: 4—6 / *Preparation time:* 20 minutes / *Cooking time:* 1 hour

Method:

1 Preheat the oven to 180°C/350°F/Gas mark 4.

2 Put the two kinds of flour and salt in a bowl and dribble 2 tbsp of the oil over the top. Rub the oil in with your fingertips until the mixture resembles coarse breadcrumbs. Slowly add anywhere from 5 to 7fl oz (150-200ml) of water and gather the flour together to form a soft doughy ball.

3 Place the dough on to a clean work surface and knead for about 10 minutes until you have a smooth and soft, but not sticky, dough. Form the dough into a round ball and rub it with about ¼ tsp oil and wrap in Clingfilm for at least 30 minutes to rest.

4 Set a large frying pan on a medium heat and add ¼ tsp of oil. Remove the dough from the Clingfilm and knead again. Separate into 12 equal sized pieces and form into circular ball shapes. Keep the others covered as you work on one at a time.

5 Take one of the balls, flatten it and dust it with some plain flour. Roll it out into a 6 inch (15cm) round, dusting your work surface with flour whenever necessary. Spread ¼ tsp of oil over the surface of the paratha and fold it in half. Repeat again with slightly less oil to form a triangle. Roll out this triangle into a larger triangle with 7 inch (18 cm) sides. Dust with flour whenever is necessary.

6 Ensure the frying pan is hot and has a light brush of oil on it before cooking your paratha. Slap the paratha on to it and let it cook for a minute. Now brush the top generously with 1 tsp oil, turn it over and cook the second side for a minute or so. Both sides should have reddish-gold spots. Move the paratha around as you cook so all ends are exposed evenly to the heat.

7 Serve as an accompaniment to any Indian dish or for dipping into hummus or other dips.

These Indian flat breads are an ideal accompaniment to any Indian dish and also great for making unique and exotic children's lunches with. Cooked directly on the pan and not in the oven they are very quick and fun to make. They are a particularly good recipe to make with children as they can get involved in the rolling out and folding of the dough to make the triangular shapes.

Chicken Hacienda

by Etta Kearney

INGREDIENTS:

4—5 chicken breasts (cut into small pieces)

8oz/225g long grain rice

1 can of chopped tomatoes

1 medium onion, chopped

1 green pepper, chopped

14oz/400g chopped mushrooms

1 tsp chopped parsley

1 tsp paprika

15fl oz/425ml chicken stock (made from two stock cubes)

Salt and pepper

Serves: 4 / *Preparation time:* 20 minutes / *Cooking time:* 1 hour

Picture the scene: the sun pours in the window, catching the bright yellow of the daffodils resting happily in the ceramic jug on the table. Atop the lace tablecloth sits a fruit bowl, full to the brim of bright green apples, juicy purple grapes and ripe bananas. This is the setting as Etta serves her husband Eddie one of his favourite dishes, bursting with flavour and spice, a little taste of Mexican sunshine at home.

METHOD:

1 Preheat the oven to 200°C/400°F/Gas mark 6.

2 In a hot oiled pan, lightly seal all sides of the chicken pieces.

3 Add the onion, peppers and mushrooms and continue to cook for another 5 minutes.

4 Add the rice, uncooked, then the paprika, parsley and some salt and pepper to taste.

5 Cover over with the tinned tomatoes and the chicken stock and bring to the boil, then reduce the temperature and simmer for around 5—10 minutes.

6 Transfer to an ovenproof or ceramic dish with a lid and bake in the oven for approximately 20—30 minutes.

7 After an hour, check to ensure there is still enough liquid remaining, add a small cup of water if not, and continue to cook for another hour.

8 Serve hot with a sprig of fresh coriander.

Masoor Dhal

(Red Split Lentils with Cumin Seed)

by Eileen D'Cruz

Ingredients:

7oz/200g red split lentils (masoor dhal), washed and drained

3 tbsp ghee or vegetable oil

2 pints/1 litre water

2 thin slices of unpeeled ginger

2 tbsp finely chopped fresh coriander

1 tsp ground turmeric

1 tsp salt

1 tbsp cumin seeds

¼ tsp cayenne pepper

A pinch of ground asafoetida (optional)

Serves: 4—6 / *Preparation time:* 20 minutes / *Cooking time:* 2 hours

Method:

1 Combine the lentils and water in a heavy saucepan and bring to a simmer. Remove any scum that collects at the top.

2 Add the ginger and turmeric and stir to mix. Cover the pan, leaving the lid very slightly ajar, turn the heat to low, and simmer gently for 1 ½ hours or until the lentils are tender. Stir every 5 minutes during the last half hour to prevent sticking.

3 Add the salt towards the end of cooking and remove the ginger slices.

4 Heat the ghee in a small frying pan over a medium heat. When hot, put in the asafoetida. A second later, put in the cumin seeds. Let the seeds sizzle for a few seconds before adding the ground coriander and cayenne pepper. Stir once and then quickly pour the contents of the pan into the pot with the lentils and stir through.

5 Sprinkle with fresh coriander to serve.

Eileen's father was with the Royal Ulster Rifles when he was posted to Karachi which is where he met and fell in love with her mother. He remained in the land of his wife's birthplace for the rest of his life. Eileen was born, educated and married in Karachi and though her father was Irish, she had never been in Ireland until the 1980's when her three brothers and her mother emigrated to Australia, but she decided to come to Ireland instead. When she first arrived on Irish shores she felt proud to be walking in her father's footsteps.

The cuisine she was brought up with greatly influences Eileen's cooking. She buys her ingredients fresh, either from the Asian market on Drury Street or from a local shop in Tallaght where they supply the spices she uses in many of her exotic dishes. She likes to create her own spice mixes and keep them handy for everyday use. She mixes coriander seed, cumin seed and turmeric, using a coffee grinder to pulverise them and adds it to many of her dishes to spice them up. Another favourite combination of hers is pepper, cinnamon, cardamom, cumin, nutmeg and cloves. She makes this spice mix to store and use over and over again, ensuring her dishes are always unique.

Masoor Dhal is a salmon coloured split pea that turns dull yellow when cooked. It is sold as 'Egyptian lentils' in some Middle Eastern stores. It is best served with a rice dish and almost any Indian meat and vegetable you like, for example: Chicken Korma or Balti.

Shahjahani Murghi

(Mughlai Chicken with Almonds & Sultanas)

by Eileen D'Cruz

Ingredients:

3lb/1.35kg chicken pieces, skinned

10 whole cardamom pods

10fl oz/300ml single cream

8—9 cloves garlic, peeled

7oz/200g onions, peeled and finely chopped

7 tbsp vegetable oil

7 tbsp plain yoghurt

6 tbsp blanched, slivered almonds

5 whole cloves

4 tbsp water

2 bay leaves

2 tsp ground cumin seeds

2 tbsp sultanas

1 inch/2.3cm stick of cinnamon

1 inch/2.3cm cube of fresh ginger, peeled and coarsely chopped

1.5 tsp salt

½ tsp cayenne pepper

¼ tbsp garam masala

This elegant, mild dish is wonderful for dinner parties. It is delicious accompanied by spiced basmati rice, cauliflower with potatoes, and yoghurt with walnuts and fresh coriander.

Serves: 6 / *Preparation time:* 40 minutes / *Cooking time:* 1½ hours

Method:

1 Put the ginger, garlic, 4 tbsp of the almonds and the water in an electric blender and blend until you have a thick paste.

2 Heat the oil in a non-stick saucepan over a medium heat and lightly brown all the chicken pieces. Remove with a slotted spoon and put them aside.

3 Put the cardamom, cinnamon, bay leaves, and cloves into the same hot oil. Stir and fry them for a few seconds. Now put in the onions. Stir and fry the onions for 3—4 minutes or until they are lightly browned.

4 Add the paste from the blender, the cumin and the cayenne. Stir and fry for 2—3 minutes more or until the oil seems to separate from the spice mixture and the spices are lightly browned. Add 1 tbsp of yoghurt. Stir and fry it for about 30 seconds. Continue doing this until all the yoghurt has been incorporated.

5 Add the chicken pieces, the cream and the salt and bring to a gentle simmer. Cover, turn the heat down low and cook gently for 20 minutes. Then add the sultanas and turn over the chicken pieces. Cover and cook another 10 minutes or until the chicken is tender.

6 Add the garam masala and stir to mix. Put the remaining almonds on a baking tray and put them under the grill until they brown lightly, tossing them frequently.

7 Remove the whole spices and any fat before serving topped with the browned almonds.

Duck in Orange Sauce
(Le Caneton á l'Orange)

—— Pauline Bradley ——

INGREDIENTS:

2 ducks (4—5lbs each)/
4 duck breasts

4 oranges

1 level tbsp caster sugar

4fl oz/125ml
red wine vinegar

10fl oz/300ml giblet
stock or chicken stock

Juice of half lemon

1 level tbsp arrowroot
or cornflour

3 tbsp Curacao

Serves: 4 / *Preparation time:* 45 minutes / *Cooking time:* 1 ¾ hours

METHOD:

1 Preheat the oven to 200°C/400°F/Gas mark 6.

2 Peel the oranges over a plate to catch the juice. Remove all pith and divide the oranges into segments. Cut the rind into strips and boil for 10 minutes in a little water. Drain and set aside with the orange segments for garnishing.

3 Place the trussed ducks on their sides in a greased roasting tin. Cook for 40 minutes then turn the ducks onto their other sides and cook for 30 minutes. After the 30 minutes place the ducks on their backs and cook for a further 30 minutes. Baste the ducks frequently with the juices in the tin throughout the cooking time.

4 Boil the sugar and vinegar together in a saucepan until reduced to a light caramel. Add the stock, reserved orange juice and the lemon juice and boil for another 5 minutes. Thicken the sauce with diluted arrowroot and stir until shiny. Strain the sauce and stir in the Curacao. Pour over the cooked duck.

5 Serve with boiled new potatoes and steamed vegetables.

Pauline was such a foodie that along with her friend Eileen she founded a club called the 1983 Club, in 1983 unsurprisingly. The club met nine times a year, each time in a different members' home, and each couple took turns to cook a new meal each time. Twice a year they went to a restaurant to do 'research'. Many, many years before the television programme 'Come Dine with Me' was even thought of Pauline and her friends had been doing just that, sharing friendship, food and new tastes with each other.

The order of business of the club was that every time the club met, three club members would each look after a course. The rule was that the chef had to stay by the stove whilst cooking and the guests were to help out in the kitchen with all the jobs, so the kitchen was always a busy fun place to be before the meal even came together. The timetable was 7pm to midnight. To mix things up another rule stood; if the club was held in your house, someone else had to be the chef so the fun of cooking a meal in someone else's kitchen always brought much fodder for the conversation at dinner. When the club met at Pauline's house, an extra guest always arrived unannounced, Trixie, the neighbour's cat would arrive at the same time as the guests and curl up in basket by the fire. When dinner was over Pauline and George would snap their fingers and say 'time to go' and the cat obediently went home. They could not always say the same for the Club members. Trixie, however, one day changed his mind after a good feed, and ending up staying for seven years!

Christmas Pudding

by Mary Lee

INGREDIENTS:

12oz/350g currants

8oz/225g raisins

8oz/225g sultanas

7oz/200g margarine

7oz/200g brown sugar

6oz/175g plain flour

2oz/50g mixed cut peel

6oz/175g fresh breadcrumbs

1oz/25g blanched almonds

2 heaped tsp mixed spice

4 tbsp beer or milk

2 eggs beaten

Rind and juice of 1 lemon

1 tbsp black treacle

2 tbsp brandy, optional

1 rounded tsp nutmeg

Serves: 10—12 / *Preparation time:* 25 minutes / *Cooking time:* 4—6 hours

METHOD:

1 Brush the inside of one large (2 pint) pudding basin with a little melted margarine. Brush a sheet of foil or double greaseproof paper with melted margarine for the top.

2 Prepare a steamer or large saucepan with boiling water on the cooker top.

3 Wash and dry the fruit and chop the almonds.

4 Melt the margarine in a saucepan. Sieve the flour, mixed spice and nutmeg together in a large mixing bowl. Add all the other ingredients and mix thoroughly into the margarine.

5 Put the mixture into the prepared basin, smooth the top, cover with the foil or greaseproof paper and tuck in securely round the rim or tie with string.

6 Place the pudding in the steamer or saucepan, cover tightly and steam over fast boiling water for 6 hours (large pudding) or four hours (two small puddings). Add more boiling water as necessary to keep the level topped up.

7 When the pudding is cooked, leave to cool, re-cover with clean greaseproof paper and store in a cool, dry place.

8 Steam again for about 1½—2 hours before serving.

9 Serve with custard or brandy sauce.

Tip: Pleat the greaseproof paper to cover the puddings before you tie it with string, to allow for expansion.

Gloriously rich and fruity, Mary's Christmas pudding was a dish that was shared with family and friends, like all good things should be. Always made well in advance of Christmas with the help and assistance of her son Alex, she used to make around nine puddings each year, one for home and the rest for her extended family. She would begin in October and make one each week. Part of her preparation was to visit family to collect the bowls from last Christmas and this meant lots of visits, chats and the gathering of news. Each pudding bore a personalised name tag and message to the recipient. The Christmas pudding routine is one of Alex's happiest memories.

CONVERSIONS

Weight

1oz/25g	8oz/225g	15 oz/425g	2lb 3oz/1kg
2oz/50g	9oz/250g	16 oz/1Lb/450g	1lb ¾/800g
3oz/75g	10oz/275g	1lb 2oz/18oz/500g	1lb 14oz/850g
4oz/110g	11oz/300g	1lb 3oz/550g	2lb/900g
5oz/150g	12oz/350g	1lb 5oz/600g	
6oz/175g	13 oz/375g	1lb 60z/625g	
7oz/200g	14oz/400g	1lb 8oz/700g	

Temperature

90°C/185°F/Gas mark ¼	130°C/260°F/Gas mark ½	170°C/325°F/Gas mark 3	220°C/425°F/Gas mark 7
100°C/200°F/Gas mark ¼	140°C/275°F/Gas mark 1	180°C/350°F/Gas mark 4	230°C/450°F/Gas mark 8
110°C/230/Gas mark ¼	150°C/300°F/Gas mark 2	190°C/375°F/Gas mark 5	240°C/475°F/Gas mark 9
120°C/250°F/Gas mark ½	160°C/325°F/Gas mark 3	200°C/400°F/Gas mark 6	

Liquid *

2fl oz/50ml	8fl oz/225ml	14fl oz/400ml	20fl oz/1 pint/600ml
3fl oz/75ml	9fl oz/275ml	15fl oz/425ml	30fl oz/1 ½ pints/850ml
4 fl oz/125ml	10fl oz/300ml	16fl oz/475ml	2 pints/1 litre
5fl oz/150ml	11fl oz/325ml	17fl oz/500ml	
6fl oz/175ml	12fl oz/350ml	18fl oz/500ml	
7fl oz/200ml	13fl oz/375ml	19fl oz/550ml	

*20 fluid ounces in an English pint

Important: This conversion table has been created for the purpose of this book and the recipes included within. It is not a universal guide and users should be aware that discrepancies and variations between measurements, temperatures and volumes may exist for the purpose of suiting a particular recipe and should be followed with care for other recipes and measurements not pertaining to this book.

INGREDIENTS:

Serves: / *Preparation time:* / *Cooking time:*

METHOD:

INGREDIENTS:

Serves: / *Preparation time:* / *Cooking time:*

METHOD:

INGREDIENTS:

Serves: / *Preparation time:* / *Cooking time:*

METHOD:

INGREDIENTS:

Serves: / *Preparation time:* / *Cooking time:*

METHOD:

INGREDIENTS:

Serves: / *Preparation time:* / *Cooking time:*

METHOD:

INGREDIENTS:

Serves: / *Preparation time:* / *Cooking time:*

METHOD:

ABOUT OUR LADY'S HOSPICE & CARE SERVICES

Our Lady's Hospice & Care Services has two truly special facilities, Harold's Cross and Blackrock Hospice, where specialist care is provided for people with a range of needs from rehabilitation to end of life care. We have wonderful staff employed in both hospices and they provide a marvellous service for patients and their families at a most difficult time in their lives. Their commitment to their work is exceptional and people get great personal satisfaction from what they do.

Being greeted with a smile each day adds to the wonderful friendliness and caring atmosphere of our facilities.

As an organisation we face many challenges in continuing to provide really high quality services for all our patients and their families. It is our intention over the coming years to develop and expand our services so that we meet the needs of our changing society while never losing sight of the core values of Our Lady's Hospice & Care Services. Our staff and volunteers understand that each person has unique needs and should be treated as an individual. The importance of the diverse cultural backgrounds and traditions of many of our staff and patients is recognised and respected.

Our Lady's Hospice & Care Services has been supported wonderfully by the public through donations, fundraising events and bequests and for this we thank you. We welcome your continued support and we would be delighted to show you our work at closer hand should you wish to visit us.

Beannachtaí agus dea-ghuí orthu siúd a thugann tacaíocht dúinn agus ar a ndéanaimid freastal, chomh maith lena gcairde gaoil.

Mo Flynn
Chief Executive Officer